F-117A
STEALTH
FIGHTER

Jane's

HOW TO FLY AND FIGHT IN THE

F-117A
STEALTH
FIGHTER

JON LAKE

HarperCollinsPublishers

9/01 LAD 4/01 23 (2)
3/06 LAD 12/02 25(2)
3/09 LAD 12/02 - 25(2)

HarperCollins*Publishers*
77-85 Fulham Palace Road
Hammersmith
London W6 8JB

First Published in Great Britain by
HarperCollins*Publishers* 1997

1 3 5 7 9 10 8 6 4 2

ISBN 0 00 470109 8

Cover painting: Iain Wyllie
Colour illustrations: John Ridyard and Chris Davey (3-view)
Editor: Ian Drury
Design: Rod Teasdale
Production Manager: David Lennox

Colour reproduction by Colourscan
Printed in Italy by Rotolito

CONTENTS

6

INTRODUCTION

8

WHY STEALTH?

14

SECRET STRIKE FORCE

32

FRONTLINE SERVICE

46

FLYING TODAY'S MISSION

88

A FUTURE FOR STEALTH?

INTRODUCTION:
THE ELITE SURPRISE

Of all the pilots in the US armed forces, those who fly the Lockheed F-117 are perhaps the most justified in thinking of themselves as an elite. Although it was conceived, designed and delivered at the height of the Cold War, when the USAF procured its aircraft in hundreds, only 59 production examples of the F-117 were ever built. The aircraft was conceived as a 'Silver Bullet', a highly specialized precision attack weapon capable of flying missions too difficult and too dangerous for any other airplane in the inventory.

Below: The F-117A is today openly flown by the 49th Fighter Wing from Holloman AFB, New Mexico, close to the White Sands National Monument, a far cry from its secret beginnings.

The aircraft was primarily intended to act as a surprise attacker, a secret strategic asset ready for use in some covert mission ordered directly by the President, perhaps one where deniability would be useful. Typical projected missions included attacks against individual terrorist leaders, or attacks on C3 (Command, Control & Communication) sites during a hostage rescue mission. Alternatively, in a real war with the Warsaw Pact, the F-117A could have flown as a pathfinder, attacking key air-defense sites to allow conventional bombers and fighter bombers to follow up with their own attacks. This would make the F-117A an effective force multiplier, making conventional fighter bombers more productive and less vulnerable. Either way, only a handful of these versatile aircraft were needed.

Pilots for this unique machine are themselves also something of a rare breed. Only a small number of pilots have ever qualified to fly the F-117, and each has been assigned a consecutive 'Bandit number' to mark his achievement. To preserve security, Bandit numbers were secret, and began at 150 for service pilots, with numbers from 100 for test pilots. In the earliest days of the program, F-117 pilots were assigned to an aircraft whose very existence was a closely guarded secret, and they could not reveal which aircraft they flew, even to their own families: they lived a strange nocturnal existence, isolated from the rest of the world. Today the existence and

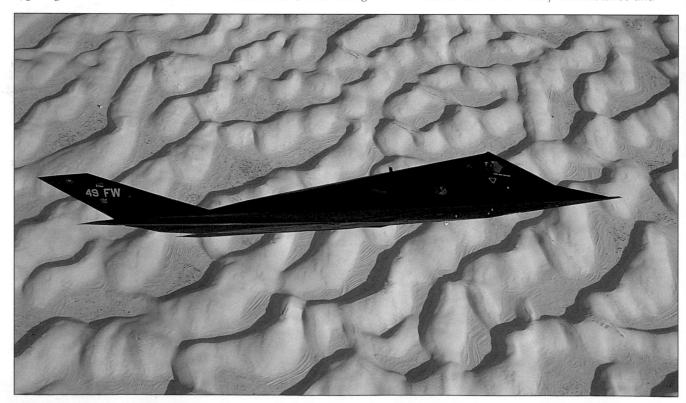

mission of the F-117 is known, but the aircraft is still surrounded by great secrecy. You need special authorization even to go close enough to the airplane to touch its strange black skin, and many of its technologies and capabilities remain very highly classified.

The F-117A has been seen in the static displays of a number of airshows in the USA and even in the UK and in Europe. But everywhere it has appeared, its groundcrew have erected barriers at least 18 feet from its wingtips nose and tail, and armed guards are there to ensure that no-one goes any closer

than that. The pilot might stand by the barrier, basking in the limelight, signing posters and programs for small boys and answering simple questions with easy charm. But start getting technical and he'll move on, or parrot a rehearsed answer which actually means nothing at all. He certainly wouldn't be willing to confirm publicly most of what is written in the pages that follow, though 95% of this information has been provided by program insiders. The US Air Force will not let the public anywhere near the F-117. This book puts you in its cockpit and lets you ride along as it flies a typical mission.

Above: Hal Farley was the pilot of the first F-117 (then known simply by its Senior Trend codename) for its maiden flight on 18 June 1981. He has since been the driving force behind the aircraft's flight test programme. His unique 'Bandit Number' reflects his unparallelled importance to the programme. He is 'Bandit 117'.

SECRET ORIGINS:
WHY STEALTH?

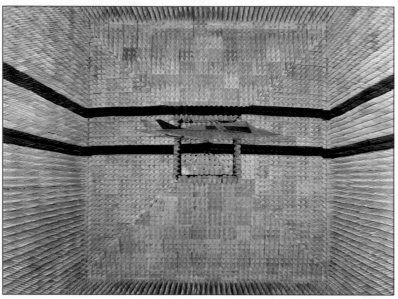

The far-sighted suggested that one such answer could lie in the reduction of the radar cross section (RCS) of tactical aircraft. This would decrease the effective range of enemy radars, potentially to a point at which interception would be impossible before the bomber reached its target. Lockheed made plans to resurrect its D-21 reconnaissance drone as the basis of a manned or unmanned attack aircraft, this vehicle having enjoyed the lowest RCS recorded to that date.

In 1975 the USAF held a Radar Camouflage Symposium at Wright-Patterson AFB, and soon afterwards, DARPA (Defense Advanced Research Projects Agency) invited Northrop, McDonnell Douglas and three other aerospace companies to design proof-of-concept stealth aircraft in a competition funded in 1976. The winner would receive a contract to build two demonstrator aircraft.

American experience in the Vietnam war and Israeli experience in the Yom Kippur war conclusively demonstrated the danger posed by increasingly sophisticated Soviet SAMs and air-defense radar. Intelligence sources indicated that the USSR would soon be deploying advanced interceptors with improved lookdown/shootdown capability. The SAM-5 was capable of reaching 125,000 ft and could be nuclear-tipped, taking care of any minor aiming errors. In the 1973 Yom Kippur war, Israel lost some 109 aircraft in 18 days, these falling to second-best export Soviet SAMs manned by ill-trained Egyptian and Syrian crews. One answer to the increasing vulnerability of tactical aircraft was to dedicate forces to electronic warfare, jamming enemy radar, or locating and directly attacking air-defense systems. But experience in Vietnam and the Middle East seemed to indicate that the allocation of resources to EW (Electronic Warfare) and SEAD (Suppression of Enemy Air Defences) was unable to halt a growing loss rate and that there had to be another, better answer.

Above left: A model of the original 'Have Blue' hangs in Lockheed's anechoic chamber, during early tests of radar cross section (RCS).

Below: Extensive use was made of sub-scale models for accurate measurement of RCS. Much of the work had to be carried out by night.

Remarkably, Lockheed were not invited to submit a design, not least because its existing Stealth experience (the SR-71 reconnaissance aircraft, the D-21 drone and the U-2, all with features to reduce RCS) was so secret that no-one actually knew their capabilities. Lockheed were able to get CIA permission to reveal SR-71 and D-21 data to DARPA, and this was impressive enough for the company to be allowed to participate in the competition. It is said that the SR-71, the size of the B-58 Hustler bomber, had a radar cross-section similar to that of the Piper Cub, about 100 times smaller than that of the contemporary F-14 fighter!

Lockheed won the competition in April 1976 with a faceted design, which proved ten times less visible to radar than that of its nearest rival, Northrop. Scale models of both were extensively tested on the radar ranges at White Sands, where it was discovered that both had lower radar cross-sections than the poles on which they were mounted! The Lockheed design's RCS was calculated as being equivalent to that of a small ball bearing, and senior Lockheed personnel lobbied air-force officers and politicians by rolling equivalent ball bearings across their desks, saying 'That's how big our new fighter bomber looks on radar!'.

Above: The Have Blue prototypes were not declassified until long after the production F-117A. Only a handful of photos of the tiny prototypes have ever been released.

Technicians make adjustments to a pole-mounted RCS model. Designing a pole with a lower RCS than the F117 was hugely difficult!

RCS tests could be disrupted by the tiniest blemish on a model's skin, from insects to bird-excrement.

THE XST PROGRAM

Above: The XSTs and the early YF-117As were shipped from Burbank to the secret test facility at Groom Lake at dead of night, aboard USAF C-5s.

When the Lockheed design's RCS was validated the whole program was reclassified Top Secret - Special Access Required, and Air Force Systems Command took over the program from DARPA, to ensure secrecy. Lockheed built two sub-scale prototypes (known as XSTs, or Experimental Survivable Test-beds) under the program name 'Have Blue'. The aircraft had no USAF serials, and no DoD designations, and remained a completely secret project. These

prototypes were quite deliberately built lightly and cheaply, using off-the-shelf components wherever possible, including J85 engines. The first prototype's role was to prove that a faceted aircraft could have acceptable handling qualities, while the second would demonstrate RCS.

The XSTs were built and test-flown in conditions of enormous secrecy. No worker was allowed to be left alone with a blueprint, and only a handful had any idea what they were working on. When the aircraft were completed, they were shipped by C-5 Galaxy to the top-secret flight test facility at Groom Lake. Here the first aircraft made its maiden flight on 1 December 1977. During this and all subsequent flights, all workers involved with other projects, and many of those working on XST itself, were locked into the mess hall. No-one who was not specifically cleared to do so was allowed to even see the aircraft. This rule was so strictly enforced that the flight test team's coffee mugs (which showed just the nose of a cartoon version of the XST, peeking from a cloud) fell foul of

GENESIS OF THE F-117

These diagrams trace the evolution of the Stealth Fighter from its origins as the sub-scale Have Blue, which represented the optimum 'Hopeless Diamond' shape to prove the LO concept.

HAVE BLUE

XST SECOND

PROTOTYPE

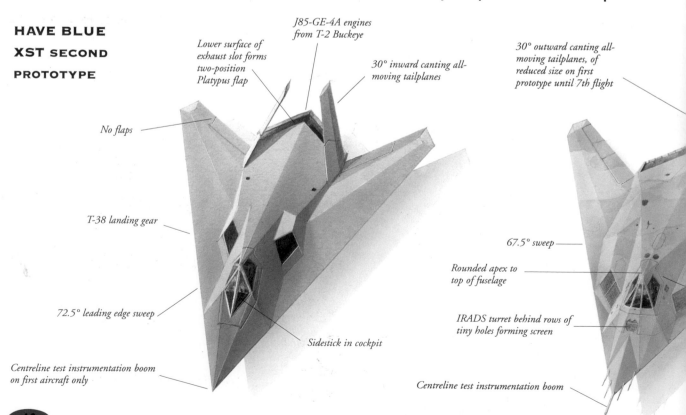

Lower surface of exhaust slot forms two-position Platypus flap

J85-GE-4A engines from T-2 Buckeye

30° inward canting all-moving tailplanes

No flaps

T-38 landing gear

72.5° leading edge sweep

Centreline test instrumentation boom on first aircraft only

Sidestick in cockpit

30° outward canting all-moving tailplanes, of reduced size on first prototype until 7th flight

67.5° sweep

Rounded apex to top of fuselage

IRADS turret behind rows of tiny holes forming screen

Centreline test instrumentation boom

Right: The prototype YF-117A takes shape at the Skunk works. The faceted nosecone has yet to be added, and the engine intakes and exhausts are completely missing. The type's conventional alloy construction is apparent.

Far Right: The wooden mock-up of the YF-117 takes shape at Lockheed's famous 'Skunk Works'. This allowed systems to be accurately positioned.

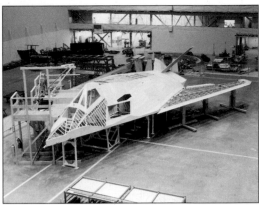

security and had to be used only in the presence of cleared personnel, and then locked securely away in a safe (not just a locked cupboard, but a steel-doored, combination-locked safe).

The XST remains an extremely secret aircraft. Both prototypes were lost in accidents, and photos of them were not released until long after the production F-117A itself emerged from the secret world. This may be because the XST's external configuration represented a closer approximation of the ideal 'Hopeless Diamond' stealth shape worked out by Lockheed, with no compromises for production or weapons system performance. It is likely that a full-scale XST would be stealthier than the F-117 as actually built.

Lockheed received an order to build a production version of the XST under the program name Senior Trend. The contract was signed on 1 November 1978, and stipulated that the aircraft would have the same RCS as the original XST wooden pole model, and that the first must fly by July 1980. The production aircraft would be a fighter-sized airplane carrying two laser-guided bombs. Five would be built initially, with twenty more to follow. Lockheed missed the contractual first flight deadline and lost $6 m on the first five aircraft. Fortunately orders totalled 29 aircraft, then 59, and the company made $80 m on the program adding in $30 m of free improvements to avoid charges of excess profit! The pre-production Senior Trend first flew on 18 June 1981.

SENIOR TREND
F-117A FIRST PROTOTYPE

PRODUCTION F-117A

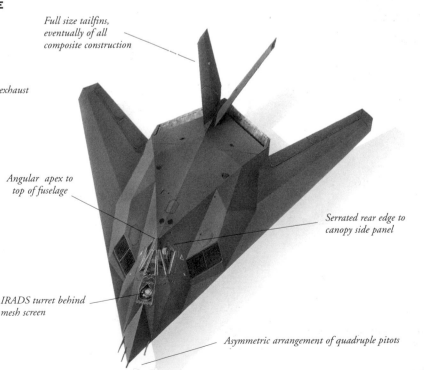

F404-GE-F1D2 engines

Fixed 'Platypus' lower surface to exhaust

Full size tailfins, eventually of all composite construction

Angular apex to top of fuselage

Serrated rear edge to canopy side panel

No serrations on rear of canopy

IRADS turret behind mesh screen

Asymmetric arrangement of quadruple pitots

NAMING THE BLACK JET

The production Senior Trend aircraft is today officially named as the Lockheed F-117A Stealth Fighter. This is a misleading epithet which takes little account of the fact that this is perhaps the aircraft in the US inventory least capable of any useful air-to-air (fighter) role. Like the F-111 before it, the F-117 is a bomber in all but name, and the fighter tag is a political convenience and an indication of the aircraft's size as much as anything else.

Below: Behind camouflage netting, Lockheed technicians and engineers prepare the first Senior Trend for its maiden flight. With panels removed, the engines can be seen, together with their jet pipes, which flattened into broad, flat slots, hidden by the upturned trailing edge.

The aircraft went unnamed for much of its early history, and there have been a confusion of designations and nicknames applied to the aircraft over the years. The name Project Harvey (after the invisible rabbit in the Jimmy Stewart film of the same name) was probably unofficial, while Hollywood also provided a nickname used by the early flight test team - 'Elliott', or 'Pete's Dragon'. It is still uncertain as to whether the COSIRS acronym (COvert Survivable In weather Reconniassance/Strike) was applied to the F-117A, or whether this was another stealth aircraft program which has remained 'black' ever since. When Lockheed gained a contract to build five FSD (Full Scale Development phase) examples of a production derivative of Have Blue (otherwise the XST, or experimental survivable test-bed) the aircraft were known by the Senior Trend program name. Senior Trend was itself a completely random codename, since although the Senior

prefix is a standard reconnaissance code word, the second word in the name was selected randomly by computer.

The first five FSD aircraft used Scorpion call signs, and were often known as Scorpions, after a Baja Scorpion successfully penetrated all the security precautions to show up on the program manager's desk! Aviation engineers and pilots are not always the world's best zoologists or entomologists and soon got mixed up as to what species the aircraft was. The name 'Cockroach' was soon used instead, especially by the less reverential service pilots. The new name stuck, since the aircraft actually looked like one! In the early days, a number of names and designations were used unofficially, including Nighthawk (which was nearly adopted as the type's official name), Ghost and Spectre, as well as the simple and straightforward Black Jet used by pilots. Outside the Stealth community, there have also been nicknames. Some applied the designation F-19, seeing a gap between the US Navy's F/A-18 and the stillborn F-20. In fact, Northrop requested the F-20 designation as a marketing ploy for their F-5G, and the gap was left deliberately. This proved extremely handy for the USAF, who could honestly deny the existence of any F-19 Stealth aircraft. For a while, after the aircraft

came out of the black world, some elements of the press called it the Wobblin Goblin, based on a misunderstood fragment of description applied to the aircraft's handling characteristics before the stability augmentation kicked in during one specific early test maneuver.

The number 117 was used before the aircraft became the F-117, the number being entered in lieu of an aircraft type on official forms and maintenance records. There have been suggestions that the designation was used to fit in with the codenames and call-sign type designations used by Groom Lake and Tonopah-based Soviet aircraft. The MiG-17 (Have Drill) was reportedly the F-113, the MiG-21 (Have Doughnut) was the F-114, while other types, including the MiG-23 and Su-7, took other designations. One story has it that the F-117A designation was reportedly adopted officially after Lockheed printed the aircraft's Dash One flight manual with F-117A on its cover. There was supposedly an unwillingness to re-print the document, even though the officially favored designation was said to have been F-19!

One thing no-one called the aircraft was the 'Stealth Fighter', since the very word Stealth had been specifically and deliberately classified as top secret, and even behind closed doors at Tonopah or within the design offices which produced the aircraft, use of the S-word was taboo. Things change, however, and once the aircraft's existence was acknowledged, the word stealth became acceptable. So officially, today, the one-time Senior Trend is the Lockheed F-117A Stealth Fighter. Although the F-117 bears the 'Lockheed' label, the aircraft was actually the product of a small and discrete division of the Californian aerospace giant, the so-called 'Skunk Works'.

Above: With extended leading edges, and with its port wingtip painted red, this is the first YF-117A, identifiable by its centreline test instrumentation boom and symmetrical pitots. The leading edge dogtooth was added late in the aircraft's career in an effort to improve take off and landing performance, and particularly to reduce landing speeds.

SECRET STRIKE FORCE:
INTO SERVICE

Today, any publication listing the order of battle of the US Air Force will openly and happily tell you that the F-117A is flown by the 49th TFW (Tactical Fighter Wing) at Holloman AFB, New Mexico, as part of Air Combat Command. With no two-seat F-117 version, its pilots tend to come from operational tours on other frontline tactical fighter types, not direct from training. There is still a requirement for a potential F-117A pilot to have 700 flying hours before conversion. This level of openness relating to the Stealth Fighter is a very new phenomenon, and is far from the situation which pertained for the first six years of the aircraft's service career, when its very existence was secret.

Below: Wearing ED (for Edwards) tailcodes, the F-117A combined test force are seen high over California. The second, third and fourth prototypes are seen with No.831, a much later aircraft used for test and trials duties.

In the early days, the F-117A was seen as an airborne equivalent to the US Army's Special Forces, or to the Navy's SEALs, with a covert 'smokeless gun' role, which might include strikes against terrorists or rogue nations on the direct orders of the President. There were plans for using the aircraft in larger, full-scale wars, but these were even more secret. Under a plan reportedly known as 'Downshift 02', for instance, it was envisaged that F-117As

might 'take out' the Dacha of the Soviet President. Complete secrecy was felt to be essential, not only to ensure surprise, but also because some operations might be deniable. The very existence of the aircraft was not admitted, and its operating unit and location had complex cover stories. While the USAF requirement stood at a single squadron of 'silver bullet' F-117As, the aircraft could have remained based at the super-secret test facility at Groom Lake, and might even have followed the U-2 and A-11 in being operated by the CIA. But when it became clear that a whole wing of Stealth Fighters would be acquired (largely due to Congressional pressure for a wing-strength unit), it was increasingly obvious that they would require a separate base. Existing airforce facilities were too well known, and too open for the new aircraft, and the decision was taken to develop an entirely new facility. For a while, there were apparently plans to base a squadron permanently in the UK (for operations in Western and Eastern Europe, the Middle East and even the USSR), with a second squadron to be based in Korea for operations in the Pacific. The third squadron would have remained in the USA for training and contingency operations in other areas. There were some plans to deploy the aircraft overseas aboard C-5 Galaxies, with their wings removed, but this was soon realized to

Above: The first prototype wore the Christian names of test pilots Farley, Anderson and Ferguson on its canopy rail.

Left and below: The first prototype was re-painted with a disruptive camouflage after its first flight in an effort to disguise its facets. The small vertical fins were replaced after Flight No.7.

be impractical, because re-assembly and re-application of RAM was too time-consuming. There was always a degree of discomfort about basing a secret aircraft at a USAF base overseas, particularly in the UK, where every airfield is closely watched by dozens of aircraft spotters, and where no airfield is really 'off the beaten track' even to the extent that major airfields in the USA often are. Macrahanish was reportedly examined as a possible base for the F-117, but in the end, it was decided that overseas operating locations would have to be just that, to preserve secrecy, and the search for a CONUS (Continental United States) base for the Stealth Fighter force continued.

HIDDEN AIRBASE

Deep in the Nevada desert, in a remote part of the Nellis AFB ranges, lay the runway for the Tonopah Test Range, one of many disused runways and airfields within the ranges. The 6,000-ft asphalt runway was originally built by Sandia National Laboratories during the 1950s to support nuclear weapons tests: the location had potential for improvement and expansion, while the only public land overlooking the base was many miles away. The airfield was subjected to a three-phase improvement and construction program.

Right: Access to sensitive areas of the secret base at Tonopah was controlled by palm-print scanners, with different categories of personnel allowed into different areas of the base, and wearing colour-coded badges.

Under Phase I, from October 1979, the base was reconstructed and expanded. The runway was extended, and taxiways, a concrete apron, a large maintenance hangar and a propane storage tank were added straight away. The USAF purchased 16 large fully air-conditioned mobile homes for a bargain $1.5 m from Chevron Oil, and these were used as dormitories while permanent accommodation was built.

Under Phase II the USAF added an extra taxiway, a new control tower, a 42,000-ft hangar, a parts warehouse, a dining hall, a water storage tank, and extensive fuel storage

Below: Armed guards surround an F-117A as it makes ready to taxy from its 'Canyon' somewhere on Tonopah's darkened ramp. Until the programme was made public, F-117As operated only by night.

tanks. Phase III saw the runway further extended to 12,000 ft (a 2,000-ft increase), and further extensions were made to the ramp and taxiways. The runway gained arrester gear, and new navigation aids were installed. More fuel storage was provided, together with LOX (Liquid Oxygen) storage, a fire station and the first individual aircraft hangars to accommodate the first 20 production aircraft. Permanent dormitories at last replaced the mobile homes, which were relegated to storage units until 1985, when all but one were removed. The remaining Chevron trailer was the TOCACL (Tonopah Officers' Club and Chinese Laundry) which was equipped with a bar, a big screen TV, pool and shuffleboard tables. By 1985 the pounding laundry machines had been moved elsewhere, and the trailer was given a much needed facelift

Below right: Tonopah's groundcrew used low-intensity 'wands' to guide the Stealth fighters from their anonymous corrugated shelters, or 'canyons'.

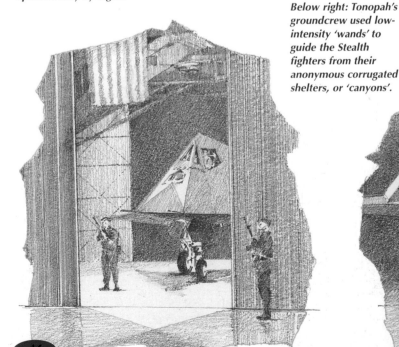

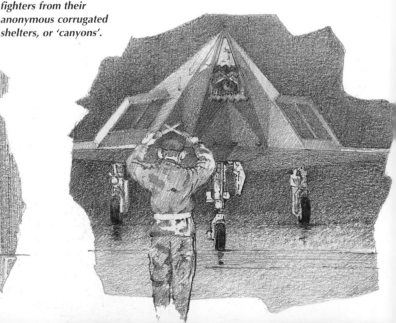

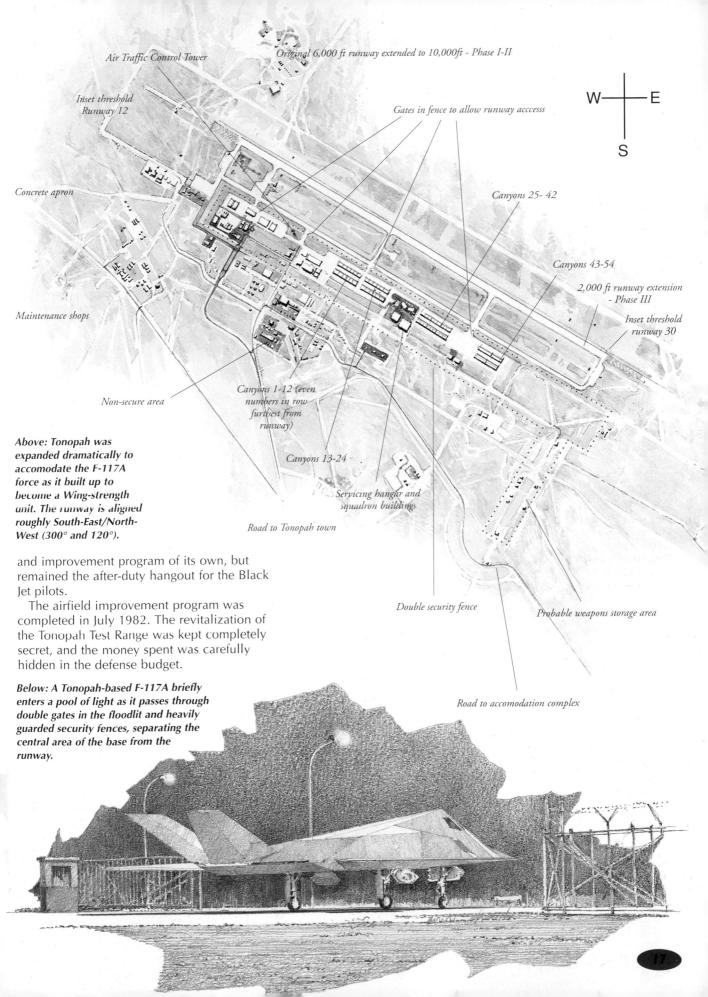

Air Traffic Control Tower

Origingl 6,000 ft runway extended to 10,000ft - Phase I-II

Inset threshold Runway 12

Gates in fence to allow runway acccesss

W — E

S

Concrete apron

Canyons 25- 42

Canyons 43-54

2,000 ft runway extension - Phase III

Inset threshold runway 30

Maintenance shops

Non-secure area

Canyons 1-12 (even numbers in row furthest from runway)

Canyons 13-24

Above: Tonopah was expanded dramatically to accomodate the F-117A force as it built up to become a Wing-strength unit. The runway is aligned roughly South-East/North-West (300° and 120°).

Servicing hangar and squadron buildings

Road to Tonopah town

and improvement program of its own, but remained the after-duty hangout for the Black Jet pilots.

The airfield improvement program was completed in July 1982. The revitalization of the Tonopah Test Range was kept completely secret, and the money spent was carefully hidden in the defense budget.

Double security fence

Probable weapons storage area

Below: A Tonopah-based F-117A briefly enters a pool of light as it passes through double gates in the floodlit and heavily guarded security fences, separating the central area of the base from the runway.

Road to accomodation complex

MYSTERY CORSAIR SQUADRON

*Left: As far as everyone outside the Senior Trend programme was concerned, the 4450th Tactical Group was a test and trials unit, nominally based at Nellis AFB, and equipped solely with the venerable A-7 Corsair. Known as the SLUF (Short Little Ugly F*****) the A-7 was the epitome of aeronautical beauty by comparison with the angular F-117A. Used for training, liaison and disinformation, the A-7s were able to visit potential operating locations by day. Significantly these included airfields in the UK, South Korea and Japan.*

It was inevitable that an entirely new unit would be formed to operate the new aircraft, since to take the identity of an existing Fighter Wing would have generated unwelcome questions. "What happened to the 4th TFW?" "What is this wing-sized unit at Tonopah?". Additionally, the new unit did not need an obvious frontline combat identity, a secondline test-unit designation fitting in far better with a number of possible cover stories.

Thus the USAF formed the 4450th Test Group on 15 October 1979, under the pretence that the new unit was an A-7 equipped unit operating in the avionics test role. It was nominally based at Nellis AFB, Nevada, where its A-7 aircraft were occasionally seen, though in reality, the unit conducted most of its operations from Tonopah. Although the existence of the 4450th Test Group was not in itself a secret, the USAF often used the meaningless designation A-Unit to further hide the operation. The Group's constituent units were originally simply numbered detachments of the 4450th TG, but they soon became numbered squadrons (flying and ground-based) and had similar, randomly allocated alphabetical alternative designations between B-Unit and Z-Unit.

The unit's A-7Ds were used as a cover for

the F-117As, to maintain flight currency before the F-117As were delivered, and before the unit had built up to full strength. The A-7D was also a useful trainer for the F-117 itself, with similar performance characteristics. In particular, prospective F-117A pilots practiced flapless landings in the A-7, to prepare themselves for the high-speed flat approach of the F-117. The aircraft were even used for miscellaneous test duties, including chase for SLCM firings. A-7 flight operations began in June 1981, by which time Britain's Prime Minister and some senior RAF officers were being kept fully appraised of the program's progress, in preparation for RAF participation and for the use of British airfields as forward operating bases. Some A-7s operated from Tonopah from the beginning, and care was taken to leave them outside the hangars, so that prowling satellites could see that Tonopah operated nothing more exciting than some clapped-out Corsairs. These aircraft were nominally based at Nellis AFB, but wore unique LV (for Las Vegas) tailcodes. There is no suggestion that this code was ever applied to the F-117As, which remained very anonymous-looking

until after they emerged from the black world.

The 4450th Tactical Group's A-7D Corsair IIs were used to conduct limited operations from potential operating locations, to familiarize pilots with bases they might eventually have to use 'for real'. In some cases, the A-7's 'role' was 'leaked'; this 'secret' cover story being that the aircraft were testing atomic anti-radar devices. The aircraft often carried black-painted modified napalm canisters, these being fitted with a red warning light, a radiation warning notice and an ominous-looking port labelled 'reactor cooling filler port'. When A-7Ds equipped with these pods visited Korea, USAF policemen closed the base, surrounding it with machine-gun-armed jeeps, and forcing groundcrew to lie face down on the ramp as the mystery A-7s taxied by.

Above: A 4450th TG pilot walks out to his F-117A at Tonopah as dusk falls. Missions were routinely carried out from inside the aircraft shelters, and not from a flightline, except for the camera!

PILOT CONVERSION

With an aircraft, a base and an operating unit designation, all that was missing was personnel. Since no-one knew about the program, there was no way of attracting volunteers, yet clearly the aircraft would demand the most highly motivated maintenance personnel and pilots. When it came to pilots, the new unit required tactical fighter pilots with sufficient experience and maturity to be able to adapt to the new aircraft, its unusual role, and the unique need for complete confidentiality. Most came from the F-4, F-111 and A-10 communities initially. Potential pilots for the program, with outstanding records and at least 1,000 hours of fighter time, were carefully screened and those who looked promising were asked whether they were interested in a job which would involve 'a great deal of A-7 flying' but without specifying what or where that job was. They were expected to make their decision within five minutes!

Below: Pilots for the F-117A trained with the 417th TFTS, previously known as Z-Unit and then as the 4453rd TES. With no dual-controlled trainer, F-117A pilots relied on groundschool and simulator training to prepare them for their first flight.

Potential squadron commanders and candidates for other senior flying appointments were even more carefully screened. Every effort was made to appoint 'fast-track' high-fliers (known as 'Fast Burners' within the USAF) who were on their way to the very top, to General rank at least. This, it was felt, would deliver two key advantages. First, the USAF would soon have a spectrum of senior officers who knew about and

understood the F-117A, and who could thus make proper use of the force. Second, the F-117A would have some powerful and influential friends.

As more pilots joined the program, the selection procedure changed slightly, with Stealth pilots themselves being asked to recommend their own acquaintances for the program. After selection, pilots were sent to the Arizona Air National Guard's 162nd TFG for conversion to the A-7D. Even after the 4450th started receiving its F-117As (beginning with 80-0787 on 23 August 1982), pilots could expect to fly the A-7 nearly as often as they flew the F-117A, and this remained true for several years. When they arrived at Nellis AFB, new personnel for the 4450th were shown into a secure lecture theatre, where they were shown a brief silent film, in which the extraordinary F-117A was seen emerging from a hangar, taxiing to the runway and taking off. 'This is what you guys will be working on", the briefing officer would say; and - to the pilots - "This is what you guys will be flying". At this point, the

suppliers, security policemen and other indirectly involved personnel would be ushered from the room, while pilots and maintainers were shown a second, more detailed, film with an informative sound track.

Before the F-117A actually entered service with the 4450th, pilots underwent ground school with Lockheed at Burbank, and were then rotated through the flight test facility at Groom Lake between 1981 and 1982 where they were briefed by Lockheed's test pilots, and where they could sit in the cockpit, and have the sensors and systems demonstrated. The first Senior Trend arrived at Tonopah on 23 August 1982, and the first flight by a TAC pilot was made on 15 October 1982. (The pilot was Major Alton C.Whitley, commander of the Tonopah-based Detachment 1 while the rest of the 4450th TG remained at Nellis, and subsequently commander of the 4452nd TS (Q-Unit), the 'Goat Suckers'). Whitley received a commemorative plaque 'In Recognition of a Significant Event, October 15 1982'. He could not tell his wife what that event was for eight years!

The first F-117As were delivered to Q-Unit, which became the 4452nd TS ('Goat Suckers') in September 1982. Later in the year, I-Unit (already designated as the 4450th TS, 'Nightstalkers') started to receive F-117s. A-7s were assigned primarily to the 4451st TS (P-Unit, 'Ghostriders'). The 4453rd TES (Z-Unit, 'Grim Reapers') activated in October 1985 and took over the training role. A final unit was R-Unit, which never received a numerical squadron designation, but which performed acceptance testing and local area familiarization flying and which parented the flight test detachment of USAF test pilots at Groom Lake and at Tonopah.

The 4450th Test Group gained IOC (Initial Operating Capability) on 28 October 1983, with the delivery of its 14th F-117A. It passed its ORI (Operational Readiness Inspection) in October 1984. The second squadron gained its IOC in the same year. There has never been a twin-stick, two-seat Stealth Fighter, although Lockheed proposed building an F-117 trainer (which would probably have become the F-117B) using the hulk of the first production F-117A, which had been written off in a pre-delivery crash. This made pilot conversion a difficult enough process, even without the further complication that all flights (even first flights) had to be made at night. Fortunately, all F-117 pilots were already experienced fast jet jockeys, and all had converted to the A-7 from their previous

type. During their A-7 training, their ability to learn and absorb information and techniques quickly was quietly analyzed. Before flying the F-117A, the pilots would fly the F-15, whose landing characteristics were said to be extremely similar to those of the F-117 itself.

The first group of potential Black Jet pilots began conversion with ten days of intensive ground school, this phase increasing steadily until the textbook and chalkboard phase lasted for several weeks. This was followed by seven sorties in the fixed-base simulator, before the so-called 'Sortie 1' which consisted of two hours going through the checklists in a powered-up cockpit. 'Sortie 2' was closer to a real flight, consisting of a high-speed taxy run, with a real brake chute deployment. This was a vital skill to learn, since in a crosswind the chute could become wrapped around a tailfin, causing damage to the skin. Until the aircraft left the black world, the pilot's first real flight in the F-117A was made (like all other flights at Tonopah) at night. An A-7D flew chase, and the pilot would get used to the aircraft's handling, usually flying some gentle aerobatics before returning to Tonopah to shoot a couple of instrument approaches. The conversion course took some five months, and included between 30 and 40 flying hours. Certain operational techniques could not be taught in the simulator, since the simulator staff were not cleared to know them, and these had to be taught on the squadrons themselves, in actual flights. After the aircraft came out of the black world conversion, training could be undertaken by day, and T-38 Talons replaced the Corsairs. On a first F-117A solo, the T-38 would take off first, flying a visual circuit and picking up the Black Jet as it climbed out, slipping into the eight o'clock position.

Above: When the F-117A emerged from the black world, Northrop T-38 Talons replaced Corsairs for training and chase duties. This aircraft of the 37th TFW wears Tonopah's TR (for Tonopah test Range) tailcode, whereas today, the 49th FW's T-38s wear an HO code signifying their base at Holloman AFB, New Mexico.

UNDER COVER OF DARKNESS

Early operations at Tonopah were extremely restricted. Although Tonopah is extremely remote, and sparsely populated, there are people in the scattered mining town nearby, and to maintain absolute security extraordinary measures had to be taken. For years, the F-117A never flew by daylight, and there was even a strict embargo on opening individual hangar doors before nightfall. If an F-117A did have to venture outside its hangar during daylight, the whole area was secured, and reference was made to a comprehensive listing of satellite overflights. If there was the slightest risk of detection, the aircraft remained under cover. Any aircraft flying near the airfield and its airspace was carefully investigated, and even trucks on nearby public roads were monitored and, if necessary, apprehended while the drivers were questioned. The base security personnel operated a fleet of UH-1N helicopters and a wide range of vehicles. Crews undergoing Red Flag exercises at Nellis were prohibited from going anywhere near Tonopah, and any who broke the rules were given a very hard time indeed on landing.

Below: Suction relief doors in the roof of each intake are open as this F-117A prepares to taxy out from its Canyon at Tonopah.

While there was no absolute prohibition on going into the town of Tonopah, such trips were discouraged, and the process was made deliberately difficult. The policy was successful: few locals had any idea what was going on at the airfield. Tonopah airfield itself was an interesting location to operate from, and the F-117As of the 4450th TG reportedly shared the base with a number of highly classified programs. For a brief period after the F-117A emerged from the black world and began flying daylight missions at Tonopah, it is said that F-117A pilots could find themselves taxying out behind the MiG-21s and MiG-23s of the 4477th Test and Evaluation Squadron - a far cry from the Luftwaffe Phantoms and Tornados with which they share their current base at Holloman AFB, New Mexico.

The 4450th Tactical Group had an unusual and unenviable working week. The pilots (apart from a handful standing alert) spent the weekends with their families at Nellis AFB, or in the nearby towns in which they had their homes. They would fly out to Tonopah aboard the chartered Boeing 727 and 737 airliners provided for the purpose, arriving at between 0800 and 0900. The 4450th TG also operated a Mitsubishi MU-2 for outside airline-hours transport of small groups of

personnel. Anybody on board one of these flights was specially cleared, some visitors to Tonopah in the early days arrived aboard UH-1 helicopters with blacked-out windows on one side, and were whisked from aircraft to ops building in a blacked-out car. Monday would be a relatively easy day, however, with an early finish to the night flying. Every effort was made to ensure that the last landing was before midnight, even during the summer months. Pilots would then fly more intensively on Tuesday, Wednesday and Thursday, returning to Nellis on the Friday. The separation from families during the week (which they were not allowed to explain) was hard enough, but the change from a primarily nocturnal existence during the week to a 'normal' existence at weekends was reportedly shattering and made it difficult to sustain a normal family life. Some felt that the posting was a guaranteed divorce, but the USAF soon stepped in to provide extra flight surgeons (a high proportion of whom were reportedly psychiatrists and counsellors) and enforce regulations relating to time off, rest hours and duty time.

F-117A pilots lived off-base, in a housing compound seven miles from the center of the airfield facilities, far enough away for aircraft noise not to be a problem to sleeping aircrew. Their accommodation had heavy black-out curtains to allow them to get proper sleep even in daylight hours. The

Right: 'Use of Deadly Force is authorised' against anyone who attempts to compromise the strict security surrounding every F-117A in service.

compounds were linked only by a shuttle bus which plied the single-track desert road by day and night. This ran almost arrow-straight to Tonopah airfield, with a gentle left hander thrown in mid-way to prevent the bus driver from falling asleep at the wheel. The bus pulled up outside the central compound, and there was no exception to the requirement that every man should clear security, each and every working day.

Above: Tonopah's corrugated Canyons were much larger than required for a single F-117A, leading many to wonder if they had been designed with a still-secret follow-on in mind, perhaps the much-rumoured 'Aurora'?

INSIDE THE COMPOUND

At Tonopah, the central rectangular compound, which contained the hangars, operations building, maintenance area and ATC tower, was bordered on all sides by double barbed-wire-topped fences. The gap between the fences was permanently floodlit, and was seeded with proximity and other sensors. The handful of entry points were heavily guarded, and each was equipped with special turnstiles incorporating palm-print scanners. A palm is as unique to an individual as a fingerprint, and comparing a print electronically with a recorded image is quicker than it would be to check papers, passes and documents manually. The scanner also allowed comparison of the relative sizes and orientation of an individual's fingers, further aiding differentiation between individuals. The palm-print scanners incorporated channels for the four outspread fingers of the right hand, with a projecting pin to be positioned between the second and third fingers. This ensured that a given hand would always be placed on a scanner in the same way, aiding the recognition process. The scanner unit incorporated a row of lights, the last two of which were a simple green (ACCESS) and a red (NO ACCESS). The only exits without turnstiles were the four to the east of the compound, leading to the runway, which were manned by armed guards, and which had massive sliding double steel gates across access taxiways.

Within the compound, personnel wore prominent 'line badges' indicating how far they were cleared into the program. A white square, for example, indicated that its wearer could see the F-117A, but could not touch it; while the green square, worn by crew chiefs and maintainers, indicated that the wearer could work on the aircraft, had a broad understanding of the aircraft's role and capabilities and understood some of its systems. Most pilots wore a black square, indicating that they had been briefed on the 'no-kidding' radar cross section (still a highly classified figure), though some had a higher category (details of the badge relating to this are, you've guessed it, still classified). These officers, who tended to be weapons instructors and senior guys involved in the development of tactics had a broader-based knowledge of the aircraft's exact capabilities, and may have been the only pilots cleared to stand alert.

Above: The 37th Fighter Wing lost its Tactical prefix on 1 October 1991, when TAC disbanded and its functions were taken over by the new Air Combat Command. This F-117A is pictured in its new markings at Tonopah during early 1992, before the move to Holloman.

Left: 'Chocks away!' In front of the aircraft, the marshaller stands ready to uncross his hands to signal 'Brakes off', once the groundcrew are clear, and the pilot is ready to taxy. For many years, hangar doors remained firmly closed during daylight hours, with complex rules and regulations as to how long after sunset doors could be opened, when aircraft could taxy, and when they could fly.

Right: When working on the F-117A groundcrew wore protective overboots to prevent damage to the RAM skin.

"SOME DAY THEY'LL KNOW"

A typical working day might begin at 1500 for a pilot assigned as mission planner on a given day. Having risen at noon, and perhaps spent an hour running or in the gym, the planner might have eaten a normal lunch before having an hour or two free. Arriving in the windowless operations building, he would pick targets and routes and nominate a realistic scenario. Normally all of the pilots flying on a particular 'wave' would fly the same route and the same mission, or one of two missions, usually simulating the same scenario. A simple navigation exercise culminating in a simulated attack on a particular dock in a Marine on Lake Tahoe, for instance, might have to be flown as though it were a strike against a target in Teheran, with all the implications that had on likely defenses, target weather conditions and the like. Often, every turn-point included a target to be located, identified, and locked onto with the IRADS. Working backwards, the planner would deconflict routes and launch times, and would then plan them in detail, preparing the tapes which the pilots would program into their computers.

Below: The aim of the F-117A's designers was to produce a shape which would present no surface at right angles to enemy radars. They achieved this through faceting.

The chow truck (like an ice cream van, but serving hot food) would come round between 1700 and 1800, allowing the planner to snatch a quick bite to eat, while pilots scheduled to fly would start to arrive. Some would sit in the ready room, with its massive wall-slogan 'Someday they'll know', while others would go to the vault in which flight manuals were kept, perhaps to learn or revise emergency procedures, perhaps just to be able to get the required 'tick in the box' for having read the Flight Manual that month. Such work was much more difficult in the F-117A community since pilots could not keep their own flight manual. The books were not allowed out of the vault, and even in the vault the manual had to be physically in the possession of the officer who'd signed it out. If he had to take a phone call, or go to the toilet, he'd first have to sign the manual back in, see it locked away, then return and go through the whole rigmarole again. At 1830 the planner would supervize a mass brief, outlining the mission, routes, required times on target, and giving actual en-route weather and a time back. The briefing would also include the simulated weather for the simulated target area, giving actual weather conditions for Teheran and its environs in our example. A simple brief might last only 20 minutes, but between 30 and 40 minutes was more normal.

Following the brief, pilots would not need to flight-plan their route formally, since they would already have a tape with the turnpoints

and timings provided by the planner. They would inevitably want to check this, however, and would want time to study their route and any target intelligence (for the actual target or targets they would be finding that night, and for the simulated Teheran target, in case of awkward questions during the debrief). They would also need to make careful notes as to their call sign, and any radio frequencies they would be using. One last-minute check before leaving operations was to ensure that the pilot was carrying a letter from the TACDO (a two- or three-star General) addressed to whom it may concern for use in the event of an unscheduled diversion and enjoining any base commander to do as he was told by the pilot carrying the letter! It is not known whether such letters were ever used 'in anger'.

With preparations complete, the first wave pilots would be driven to the individual hangars accommodating their assigned aircraft. At Tonopah the hangars were arranged in blocks of six, six, nine and six per row, in two close parallel rows. Those closest to the runway bore odd numbers, from 1 to 53, while those in the rear row were even-numbered, from 2 to 54. The first 24 hangars differed slightly from the next 18, having vents on their roofs and with concertina-type doors. These differed from the first batch of

shelters in having sliding panel doors in eight sections, and themselves differed from the last 12 hangars. The overall effect was one of uniformity, however. All were constructed from corrugated steel sheet, and all were painted in a pale sandy color, with an identical black number board on the left hand edge of each door. All had identical clean white floors with neatly painted taxi guidelines, and a parking point (with full latitude and longitude) indicated to allow absolute precision when aligning the INS.

Above: The DLIR sensor can be seen below the nearest of these two F-117As, to the right of the nosewheel, ahead of the red anti-collision light.

Below: The Sandia National Laboratories airstrip at Tonopah was transformed into a modern air base for the F-117, in utter secrecy.

TAKE OFF

Arriving at the correct shelter, the F-117A pilot entered through a small personnel door, going into the hangar through a small unlit annexe. This meant that no light showed when the small door was opened. The main hangar doors remained firmly shut until official twilight (half an hour after official sunset), with official twilight, sunset, and moonrise charts being consulted to determine the time at which doors could be opened. Some reports suggest that this prohibition was backed up by the use of a sensor which could detect when no direct sunlight was hitting the unit. This was used to confirm the official sunset time. In addition to these precautions, it was ruled that from two hours after sunset until two hours before sunrise, the hangar lights had to be turned off whenever the doors were opened, however briefly.

Above: The pilot of the F-117A has his view of the outside world severely constrained by the heavily-framed canopy. The pilot of this Stealth Fighter wears the insignia of the 57th Fighter Wing on his shoulder. This Nellis-based unit conducts weapons, and tactics training and development and incorporates a 2-3 aircraft F-117A element.

The first wave might typically begin to take off at 2100, and all 12 aircraft would have departed by 2300. With a typical 90-minute sortie time, the aircraft would land between 2230 and 0030 and a second wave would take off from 0000 to 0100, landing between 0130 and 0230. Within about 35 minutes of landing, the F-117A pilot would be back in the Operations Building, ready to debrief.

Although Tonopah had a small control tower, it was not too hard-worked. Even when F-117As going off range communicated with other agencies pretending to be A-7Ds, they usually operated 'radio silent' at Tonopah itself. The most important role for Tonopah's

air-traffic controllers was to monitor the airspace surrounding the base for intruders!

The planner would be among the last to leave after the last aircraft had landed, since he would also act as a flying supervisor and might be required to debrief the returning pilots, going over their tapes with the squadron's weapons officer. On Thursdays, everyone would tend to retire to the TOCACL after the end of flying, to have a beer and watch the sun-up, before returning to the accommodation annex to get ready for the Key Airlines flight back to Nellis. On Mondays, Tuesdays and Wednesdays, (with flying the next night) pilots might also have a beer at the TOCACL, but were far more careful to get back to their beds before the sun rose. During the week, Tonopah was often likened to a Vampire Convention, with personnel rushing to hide themselves before they could be touched by the sun's rays. This was an essential precaution, since the human mind will not allow the body to rest properly once it has seen daylight, 'knowing' that it should be active. The Tonopah working week was hard enough, without risking disrupted sleep patterns.

Black Jet pilots typically logged between ten and twelve F-117A flights per month, with

Left: A pair of F-117As taxy out at Tonopah. The aircraft's flattened, shell-like fuselage and primarily nocturnal habits led some to apply the unflattering nickname 'Cockroach'. The F-117A proved similarly elusive, but very much more deadly. The F-117A normally operates alone, and formation sorties (even by as few as two aircraft) are exceptionally rare.

Below: One F-117A takes off from Tonopah as another sits on Tonopah's taxyway. The Stealth Fighter's take off performance is adequate, though without afterburner, it is never spectacular. The basic F-117A carries only a relatively small payload, a pair of 2,000 lb LGBs, or less.

five or six further missions in the A-7. Virtually all flight time was spent practicing realistic operational profiles, though there was little opportunity for the dropping of live ordnance, since few ranges were active at night and use of the laser 'off-range' was prohibited. On the rare occasions that live ordnance was dropped, the 4450th made use of the same 'broadband, wide-spectrum, inexpensive, expendable point-source target' invented by the flight test team at Groom Lake - a barrel filled with glowing charcoal! In-flight refuelling was a vital element in Black Jet operations, and was therefore practiced more often, with each pilot able to practice refuelling once a week. Weather had a disproportionate effect on F-117A operations, with snow or a full moon preventing the aircraft from flying 'off-range' at all, and with even 50% moonlight closing many of the approved 'off-range' training routes. The risk of hail (which would have damaged the aircraft's RAM) was enough to keep aircraft firmly under cover. In the very earliest days, weather had an even greater effect, since early aircraft had unheated pitots, so were prohibited from flying in cloud, or when icing was predicted.

ON THE PRESIDENT'S ORDERS

Once sufficient aircraft were available, some 12 F-117As were maintained on standby, ready for any mission ordered by the President. Two aircraft were ready to go at a mere two hours' notice. But while the aircraft were ready to undertake any mission, the order to go was never given. Twice aircraft were armed for strikes and pilots were briefed, but on each occasion the missions were scrubbed before takeoff.

Above: An F-117A over one of the aircraft's most frequent training targets, Lake Tahoe. Marinas and even individual boats presented difficult targets, with little difference in IR signature to the surrounding water. No.802 was the 18th production F-117A, and was named 'Black Magic' during the Gulf War.

During October 1983 F-117's were considered for use in support of the US invasion of Grenada (Operation Urgent Fury) but were judged not ready according to some reports. During the same month several F-117As (variously reported as five, seven or ten) had their INS equipment fully aligned ready for a strike against PLO targets in the Lebanon. It was planned that the aircraft would fly to Myrtle Beach, where they would land and refuel, and where the pilots would have a face-to-face brief with their tanker crews and the pilots of 'other support aircraft'. Four aircraft (plus air

spares) would then have flown direct to the target. The mission was cancelled only 45 minutes before the planned takeoff. It has also been reported that another operational mission was planned in 1983 by Lt Col Oliver North. This would have reportedly involved a strike against Colonel Gaddafi by F-117As operating from Rota in Spain. On 15 April 1986 an unknown number of F-117As were readied for participation in Operation El Dorado Canyon, the retaliatory strike against Colonel Gaddafi following Libyan military actions against US Navy ships in the Gulf of Sidra and Libyan-sponsored terrorist outrages against US targets. In the event, the mission was not regarded as being important enough to risk compromising the F-117A, and their takeoff was cancelled one hour before it was due to take place. The raid was flown by carrier-borne strike aircraft and UK-based F-111Fs.

Although F-117As did not undertake operational bombing missions before 'coming out of the black' there is plenty of circumstantial evidence to suggest that they may have deployed to overseas OLs (Operating Locations). There were widespread reports that British enthusiasts heard an aircraft declare an emergency and divert to RAF Lakenheath, where the roads round the base were rapidly closed by USAF policemen just before a 'strange sounding' machine landed. This was apparently put straight into a shelter, departing some nights later, when roads were again closed. Other reports suggested that the aircraft operated from Alconbury, Sculthorpe and Wethersfield (all RAF stations accommodating USAF units) and Binbrook, an RAF fighter station. The Binbrook 'rumor' was more detailed than most, with suggestions that the F-117A would take off in close formation with a based Lightning (which would explain night-time aircraft noise and provide a radar blip) before flying off on a representative sortie profile along (or even just over) the Iron Curtain, testing the aircraft against the latest Soviet air-defense systems. The inclusion of an RAF exchange officer in the program gave credence to these rumors, since RAF officers in the U-2 (and possibly in the SR-71 and RB-69 programs) won their places as reciprocation for the use of British bases. In the case of the U-2, RAF and CIA pilots made the crucial overflights of the USSR, which USAF U-2 pilots were not permitted to fly.

An F-117A cruises over high clouds. Even in the invisible-to-radar F-117, the wise pilot would avoid flying immediately above or below unbroken cloud, against which he might be silhouetted.

Above inset: The red-outline on the rear underfuselage of the F-117A surrounds the bay for the arrester hook, which has to be deployed explosively, and is an 'emergency only' piece of kit.

Right: An unusual side-on view showing typical toned down markings, with a simple three-digit serial, the TAC badge (until 1981) and a wing badge on the intakes.

FRONTLINE SERVICE: STEALTH GOES PUBLIC

Below: A Tonopah-based Stealth Fighter flies over the Half Dome in Yosemite National Park. Daylight flights were virtually unheard of during the early days of the programme.

By 1988, the F-117A's Black status was seriously restricting operations. More serious than the inability to fly by day was the impracticality of operating alongside other units (since to do so would have compromised security). Even in-flight refuelling was difficult, since only a handful of tanker crews from two refuelling wings (at March and Beale) were let into the secret and cleared to refuel the Stealth Fighter. Moreover, rumors of strange aircraft flying in Nevada were growing stronger.

The F-117A finally 'came out of the closet' on 10 November 1988, when the Pentagon released a single, heavily distorted, retouched, and electronically altered photograph. Lockheed joined in the fun by releasing a piece of artwork based on the photo, in which the facets were more apparent (though completely altered in alignment) and with a tiny pilot in the cockpit which made the aircraft look B-52 sized! This allowed a change in operating procedures, including limited daylight flying and participation in exercises. The possibility of daylight operations had an immediate effect on the training and conversion process, meaning that F-117A pilots no longer had to

Below: The 4450th Tactical Group became the 37th TFW in 1989.

make their first flight in the aircraft in darkness. The ageing A-7s were replaced in the chase role by cheaper-to-operate T-38s from January 1989, the latter being assigned to the 4453rd TS, while the A-7-equipped 4451st TS ran down. The 4452nd TS inactivated on 30 May 1989, while the R-Unit inactivated the same day, continuing to operate at Tonopah as an undesignated subordinate of the 6510th Test Wing. More photos of the aircraft (taken by intrepid photographers who trekked out into the desert) soon emerged. These revealed many new features, among which was the adoption of unit markings by the Black Jets. Before their existence was revealed, the aircraft flew with a three-digit serial on the tailfin, and a low conspicuity rendition of the Tactical Air Command badge on the fin tips. Some aircraft also had a 4450th TG crest on the engine intakes. Now the aircraft had prominent white 'TR' tailcodes, and Group and Squadron markings became more common.

On 5 October 1989, the unit took a further step into the 'normal' world, when it adopted the designation and traditions of the 37th TFW, an F-4G Phantom Wild Weasel wing, which had just disbanded at George AFB. The re-designated Stealth unit remained at Tonopah, however. The 4450th's surviving three squadrons were redesignated, with the 4450th TS becoming the 415th TFS, retaining its 'Nightstalkers' name and badge. The 4451st TS (hitherto an A-7 unit) gained F-117As and a new designation as the 416th TFS, 'Ghostriders'. The 4453rd TES became the 417th TFTS (Tactical Fighter Training Squadron) 'Bandits'.

TARGET PANAMA

On 19 December 1989, the 37th TFW finally took the F-117A into action for the first time. Six F-117As took off to attack two sets of targets in Panama during the US operation to topple Noriega. Two of the aircraft turned back when the attack on their targets was cancelled (they had been assigned to support special operations forces who hoped to capture Noriega himself, and the mission was cancelled when it became clear that he could not be located). Two more aircraft flew only as air spares. The final two aircraft attacked barrack buildings near Rio Hato, with the stated aim of dropping bombs near enough to stun and disable the defenders, but without either destroying the buildings or causing major casualties.

Above: Six F-117As took off from Tonopah to participate in 'Just Cause', the operation to topple Panama's dictator Noriega.

Below: Three F-117As lined up outside Canyons 1, 3, and 5 at Tonopah.

This unusual mission was intended to minimize casualties among parachute-landing US troops from the 2nd and 3rd Ranger Battalions. Unfortunately, a last minute change of plan led to the lead pilot dropping his single GBU-27 bomb where the second aircraft should have aimed (while also failing to compensate for the wind), while the second pilot's aim point was an unspecified point a set distance and bearing from the first aircraft's

bomb. Once the first bomb went awry, the second was bound to be even further off-target.

Instead of generously missing two barrack buildings the two GBU-27s narrowly missed a third barracks, generating a fireball which gutted it and destroyed an empty cantina. The accuracy of the bombs was further hampered by the poor performance of the F-117A's IRADS sensor, which was hampered by the humidity and vegetation in the target area, which lowered contrast to a barely acceptable level. There were those who questioned whether an F-117A was strictly necessary in order to guarantee a hit on an empty field (let alone to miss its target within that field!), and there were criticisms that the raid had been 'unnecessary show-biz' designed primarily to win funding for the program. Others felt that the use of the F-117A had been justified by the need for bombing accuracy, and by the desire to minimize collateral damage. The

truth is probably that the aircraft had to be used in Panama, mainly so that Congress could actually see some return from the Black Program which they had unwittingly been funding for so long, but which they now knew about.

At the end of the day, however, the F-117A mission was judged a success by the 'customer', and the Rangers' commander judged that the aircraft's bombs did cause confusion among the defenders, and did save lives on both sides. Fortunately, the F-117A's next combat experience was altogether more successful.

Above: The pilot of the F-117A has a vital if unglamorous role, for he is the unseen assassin, using the cover of night to attack his target undetected.

BLACK JET IN THE GULF

Above: On 19 August 1990, en route to the Gulf, the 22 F-117As of the 415th TFS (including four spares) made a refuelling stop at Langley AFB, Virginia, where the pilots grabbed a night's rest before crossing the Atlantic and flying on to 'Tonopah East', a newly rebuilt and modernised airbase near Khamis Mushayt in Saudi Arabia.

When Saddam Hussein invaded neighboring Kuwait, the international community was remarkably unanimous in its condemnation of his actions. Even more remarkably, the USA was able to organize a relatively large coalition of countries prepared to use military force, initially to try to intimidate the Iraqis to withdraw, and later to actually force them out of Kuwait. It was clear that a straightforward direct attack on Iraqi forces in Kuwait was not the best way of achieving the coalition's aims, since such an attack could have resulted in massive casualties among the Iraqis in their prepared defensive positions, and might have wreaked terrible destruction on Kuwait itself. It was felt that a heavy but limited blow against Iraq's military machine and command infrastructure could prevent the reinforcement of the forces in Kuwait. This strategy would also allow a targeted offensive, preventing Iraq from continuing its occupation and resisting allied operations, while simultaneously destroying the will to fight.

But the coalition was a fragile one, and it was apparent from the start that every effort would have to be made to keep casualties on both sides very low, and to minimize collateral damage. Seeing US servicemen being brought home in body bags would have rapidly wiped out public support for the operation. It was clear that any military campaign would have to be limited in duration and extent, to avoid claims that the war was being fought for control of oil in the region, and not simply to right a wrong. To have killed large numbers of enemy civilians, or to have destroyed a religious building would have handed Saddam Hussein victory in the propaganda war, and might have made it difficult to keep some Arab members of the coalition 'on board'.

These unusual requirements dictated that the military campaign to oust Iraqi forces from Kuwait would have to be undertaken with speed and with surgical precision. General Chuck Horner's plan envisaged the destruction of 84 key targets in the first week

Above: The 415th TFS lined up at Langley AFB, the largest gathering of F-117As ever seen outside Tonopah, and perhaps the largest number ever seen in the open, on the ground, at once.

Right: Colonel Al Whiteley, CO of the 37th TFW during Operation Desert Storm.

of air operations - a highly ambitious aim. It was obvious that the F-117A would be an extremely useful tool in any such campaign, since it offered the potential ability to tear out the eyes, ears and heart of Iraq's military machine. Accordingly, the USAF deployed the 415th TFS to Khamis Mushayt in Saudi Arabia, 900 miles from Baghdad (as the crow, but not the military airplane, flies). The deployment began at 0645 on 19 August, when three cells of twelve KC-135s took off from Beale AFB, California. At 0800 the 22 F-117As joined the tankers and flew on to Langley AFB, Virginia, refuelling three times on the way. The Black Jets night-stopped at Langley, while the KC-135As flew on to Saudi Arabia, waiting only for three aircraft which had landed at Plattsburgh after heavy crosswinds forced a refuelling stop. The next day, the F-117As flew to Saudi Arabia themselves, accompanied by KC-10A Extenders from March AFB. This non-stop flight took 15 hours, and was a severe test of the endurance of aircraft and aircrew alike.

TONOPAH EAST

The Saudi airfield had many parallels with the F-117's home base, located in a similar desert and at a similar elevation (6,776 ft for Khamis, 5,500 ft for Tonopah). When they arrived, the Black Jets occupied brand-new shelters very similar to those they had left behind in Nevada, but each accommodating eight aircraft in four bays, parked nose to tail. The front aircraft would be towed outside to start, but the second could start up within the canyon itself. The shelters were fully hardened and were serviced by revetted taxiways. The quality of the facilities was hardly surprising, since the base had been rebuilt by the USA during the early 1980s, with extra shelter areas provided to support deployments by USAF units. The shelters used by the 415th TFS actually still had seals on their doors. Inevitably, the Saudi base came to be nicknamed 'Tonopah East'.

Far right: The shelters and taxyways at King Khalid air base, Khamis Mushayt, were well protected against air attack, with reinforced concrete covered and camouflaged with rocks, and with plentiful revetments. The shelter areas were far more like real canyons than the so-called Canyons at Tonopah.

Below: Two of the 42 F-117As deployed to Khamis Mushayt being prepared for a mission outside their shelters. Late in the war it was apparent that the risk of air attack by Iraq was negligible, and aircraft occasionally operated from flightlines.

If anything, the F-117 pilots actually enjoyed better facilities at Khamis than they had at Tonopah. They slept, four to a room, in bedrooms attached to the shelters, each of which had a massive generator, with facilities for over-pressurization in the event of NBC (Nuclear, Chemical or Biological) contamination outside.

The F-117As were operational by 26 August, and the unit began intensive training, until the process of briefing, starting and flying to the tanker drop-off point was second nature to every pilot. The unit also got its logistics and maintenance organization up and running very quickly. Having deployed with extra spares in the shape of war readiness spares kits, a repair program for avionics units was instituted while the squadron's avionics maintenance vans were still en route to the Gulf. Aircraft were also cannibalized for spares when necessary, resulting in a readiness and serviceability rate which was actually higher than was normal back home at Tonopah.

TARGET BAGHDAD

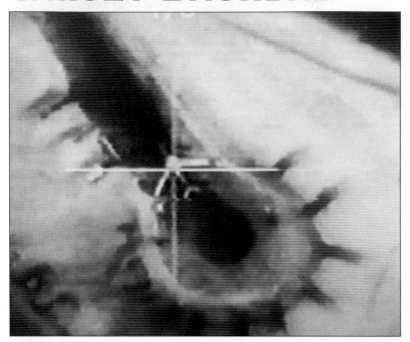

The US Studies and Analysis Agency produced detailed computer models based on General Chuck Horner's plan for the campaign, and these showed that non-stealthy warplanes would suffer unacceptably high losses if they attempted to hit targets in the Iraqi capital, and even predicted that numerous F-117As would be shot down before they reached their targets. This was a serious finding, and prompted the development of complex plans for the bombing of F-117A wreckage if any aircraft had been downed. This was felt to be the best way of ensuring that the aircraft's secrets would not be compromised. Some urged the development and incorporation of 'self-destruct' systems similar to those developed for the U-2, for activation by the pilot on ejection, but this was not felt to be practical or desirable. But if the F-117A was felt to be vulnerable to hostile defenses, it was considerably less vulnerable than any other type, and it was allocated the most important targets. Within a month of Dugan's outburst it was confirmed that the F-117A and unmanned cruise missiles would be the only weapons used against Baghdad itself.

Half of the problem was that the very secrecy which had kept the F-117's capabilities hidden from potential enemies had meant that its own commanders knew too little about the aircraft and how it could be best used. The Desert Storm air commander, General Chuck Horner, was initially apprehensive as to how the aircraft might shape up in combat. "We had a lot of technical data, but I had no way of knowing that we would not lose the whole (F-117) fleet that first night of the war. We were betting everything on the data proving the technology - but we had no real experience with the airplane to know for certain how well it performed under fire. We sent those boys in naked and all alone. As it turned out, the data was right on the mark. But we should've known that before the first attack." In Horner the USAF had a gutsy commander prepared to take the risk.

In early November, the USAF decided to deploy a second F-117A unit (the 416th TFS)

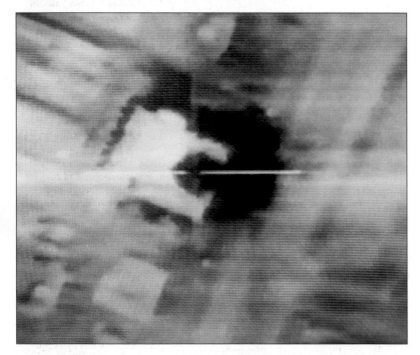

Following a September 1990 visit to the F-117A force at Khamis Mushayt, the air-force Chief of Staff General Dugan opined that the air campaign's "cutting edge would be in downtown Baghdad", and hinted that Saddam himself would be a key target. This was an extremely accurate prophecy, but to admit that the enemy leader would be personally targeted was unacceptable, and earned Dugan a summary dismissal. The capabilities and effectiveness of Iraq's air-defense system were consistently overestimated during Operation Desert Shield, and no-one seemed able to predict the level of dislocation that would be caused by first night strikes against it.

to Saudi Arabia, as it became increasingly clear that Saddam would not be backing down. The Ghostriders finally arrived in theatre on 4 December 1990, leaving only a skeleton training force at Tonopah under the 417th TFS. As the role to be played by the Black Jet increased, support assets increased proportionately. Initially, the KC-135s from Beale AFB were assigned as the F-117A's in-theatre tankers, but these were joined by the KC-135Rs from the AFRes tanker unit at Grissom AFB, Indiana.

On 16/17 January 1991, the first night of Desert Storm, the 415th and 416th TFS launched two waves of F-117As against Baghdad. The first was led by the 415th's CO, Lt. Col. Ralph Getchell, while Al Whitley, CO of the 37th and de facto detachment commander, led the second. The enemy AAA barrage over Baghdad was incredibly spectacular, while SAMs were being fired in huge numbers. Many of the F-117A pilots flying over Baghdad that night were quite convinced that their number was up, and more than one dreaded returning to Khamis Mushayt as the sole survivor of the evening's effort, so convinced were they that no-one could survive in the maelstrom of fire. Of 65 F-117A pilots deployed, only four had any combat experience, and one of them had only one combat mission to his credit. Even the old hands, including Wing Commander Colonel Alton Whitley, who had flown combat missions over Vietnam, found the intensity of the Iraqi flak quite incredible. But while the barrage of AAA looked impressive, it was entirely blind, and was ineffectual. Not one F-117A was hit on that or any other night. Nor did the barrage force the F-117As to drop their bombs wildly or inaccurately, which was its primary purpose. But the pilots were not to know any of that. After the war Getchell affected a studied nonchalance: "Most of the guys figured that since we'd already been in Saudi Arabia for six months, and in the air for a little over two hours, it would be kind of foolish to turn around and go back, so we went ahead." This was actually heroism of the highest order (since most pilots admitted to fear, which they overcame), and it must have felt like flying into the dragon's jaws. The list of targets hit by the Black Jets during their first night of operations is quite frightening.

The first wave of Black Jet targets hit in Baghdad included the 370-ft Al Quark communications relay tower (attacked by Capt.Marcel Kerdavid, who won the Silver Star for this attack and his subsequent attack

on the National Command Alternate Bunker at North Tajii), the Al Karak main telephone exchange, colloquially known as the AT&T building (Captain Paul Dolson), the Iraqi air-defense headquarters (Captain Mark Lindstrom), and the National Air Defense Operations Center (Lt.Col. Ralph Getchell). Moments later, more F-117As attacked. Major Jerry Leatherman, for example, aimed two GBU-10s through the hole in the roof of the AT&T building punched by Dolson's GBU-27A/B penetrator. Lee Gustin wrecked the presidential palace east of Baghdad's airport. Pilots who still carried a bomb went on to attack other targets, with Kerdavid attacking the National Command alternate bunker at North Tajii, with little apparent effect. The same target was attacked twice more by F-117As, then was finally taken out by F-111Fs later in the war, using specially developed bunker-busting bombs.

Above: Stress is clearly etched in the face of this F-117A pilot. In the early days, the intensity of the barrage of AAA and SAMs led many Stealth pilots to wonder if they could possibly survive. It soon became clear that Baghdad's defences were firing blind, however.

Below: Jokey messages were de rigeur on bombs dropped on Iraqi targets. These reflected the high morale among USAF armourers, and perhaps a subconscious desire not to think too much about the deadly purpose of such lethal ordnance.

BUNKER BUSTING

Left: The F-117A used two types of weapon during the Gulf War, both 2,000-lb LGBs. This is a GBU-27, before installation of the Paveway III guidance kit.

But before the main force of F-117s reached Baghdad, other Black Jets added to the mayhem and confusion, initially striking the intercept operations center near Nukhayb (which controlled the fighters at H1 and H2 airfields), and the sector operations center at H-2, near Ar Rutba, in Western Iraq. Both of these targets were hit by the same pilot. Major Greg Feest, the man who dropped the first bomb in Panama dropped the first bomb of the Gulf War, too, watching as the doors blew off the Nukhayb bunker before turning towards his second target. This effectively put the southern fighter bases out of action, and further deprived Iraqi air force and air-defense chiefs of information. Moments later, Captain Blake Bourland sent the Sector Operations Center at Tallil off-line. The war had begun with attacks by US Army AH-64 Apaches and US Marine AH-1 Cobras on surveillance radar sites close to the border, effectively punching two huge holes in the border defenses, through which strike aircraft (including the F-117As) began to pour. Cruise missiles had then attacked communications relay and power stations in Baghdad, waking the defenses.

Even after the Black Jets left Baghdad, and even after a second wave of cruise missiles targeted against ministry buildings and telephone exchanges, the Iraqi air-defense system remained in reasonable shape. US Navy A-6s and F/A-18s launched some 137 TALDs (simulating full-sized attack aircraft) at Baghdad, and these were mostly engaged and destroyed by the defenses, though in doing so, they marked themselves for destruction by a massive force of 'Wild Weasel' F-4G Phantoms and F/A-18 Hornets.

The second wave of F-117As which attacked on the first night re-visited the Air Force Headquarters and the National Air Defense Operations Center, while other SOCs elsewhere in the country were taken out by the Black Jets. Many senior Iraqi air-force and air-defense officers were killed during the attacks. Of the survivors, more were executed because of the dismal performance of the system they controlled.

The 37th TFW soon ran out of strategic targets, and was soon allocated tactical targets, from Iraqi aircraft sitting on the ground (reportedly including one of the scarce Adnan AEW aircraft and a group of Tu-16 bombers being readied for an attack using chemical weapons), to captured Kuwaiti HAWK SAM sites and Iraqi hardened aircraft shelters.

Despite the fact that it provided only 2.5% of the 'shooters' in theatre on day one of Desert Storm, the 37th TFW hit 31% of the first night targets. During the war as a whole, the force flew 1,271 combat sorties and over 6,900 combat flying hours, carrying 2,567 bombs to their targets. These scored 1,669 direct hits, and 418 misses, though there were also 480 no drops due to weather. In doing so, it was claimed that the Black Jet had "demonstrated a level of accuracy unmatched in the history of air warfare". Not a single F-117A was even touched by enemy air defenses. Some other coalition aircraft enjoyed very low loss rates, but none were sent into the teeth of such danger. Perhaps most importantly, collateral damage was insignificant. Military facilities were obliterated without touching nearby mosques, and throughout the war, the civilian population felt safe enough to walk the streets.

TAC's commander, General John Loh, told the US Senate that the F-117A had been eight times more efficient than non-Stealth warplanes in putting its bombs on target. Congress urged the USAF to cancel its requirement to buy an additional 72 F-16s, and to buy 24 new F-117As instead, but the plan came to naught, probably because the very success of the aircraft was starting to threaten planned future programs. The big worry was that Congress might say, "If the F-117 can do all this, why do you need JSF, or

JAST, or whatever?" It was not an easy question to answer. Senior figures began to run down the F-117A, with Horner's Gulf War deputy, General Buster Glossom, charging that the F-117A represented "archaic, 15 year-old technology" that was "a nightmare to maintain". Lockheed themselves were carefully warned that lobbying for a re-opening of the F-117A production line would be a threat to their own F-22.

Above: The F-117A demonstrated incredible levels of accuracy, and delivered its deadly weaponloads without requiring massive fighter or SEAD support. This made it a particularly economic means of attacking enemy targets.

Left: An F-117A taxies out for a mission as dusk falls. The aircraft carried all of its fuel and ordnance internally, to preserve its low radar cross section. Late in the war, the ability to carry a higher payload externally would have been valuable.

Right: One by one, Iraq's airfields were attacked and turned into ruins. Here hardened aircraft shelters have been attacked using LGBs, blowing off their doors. The F-117A attacked air defence installations, bunkers and bridges, among a long list of targets.

RETURN TO IRAQ

The wing, and its squadrons, finally lost the Tactical prefix on 1 October 1991. Between 9 May and 7 July 1992 the F-117A took another step out of the secret world when it moved from its specially built Tonopah base to Holloman AFB, New Mexico, next to the White Sands National Monument and close to the town of Almagordo.

Above: An F-117A returning to Langley AFB after the Gulf War. The pilots of the 37th TFW returned to a heroes' welcome, and with Lockheed's extravagant claims for their aircraft thoroughly vindicated. Despite its success, the aircraft remains a rarity in USAF service, and no further procurement is likely.

The move to Holloman was accompanied by a further change of unit designation, with the 37th FW becoming the 49th FW, previously equipped with F-15s at Holloman. It was ostensibly made as a "further step to integrate the F-117A into everyday operations", though the truth may be less prosaic. There seems little doubt that Holloman is less well suited to Stealth Fighter operations, with inferior facilities, and this has had an impact on readiness and sortie rates. After the F-117As left Tonopah, security around the base actually increased. In any case, it seems inconceivable that Tonopah, the USAF's newest air base, has been left empty so the question has to be asked - what has replaced the F-117A at Tonopah?

Although the F-117A squadrons from

Tonopah initially retained their numerical identities after the move to Holloman, all were eventually re-designated, using the identities of the units which had traditionally constituted the 49th. Thus the 415th FS became the 7th FS , the 416th FS became the 8th FS, and the 417th FS became the 9th FS. There was reportedly fierce resistance to the loss of the squadron designations under which the Black Jet had gone to war.

The 8th FS has the 'Pacific Contingency' responsibility, and would deploy to South Korea in time of tension. The 7th FS has what is known as the 'Atlantic Contingency' and would deploy to Europe or Saudi Arabia if required. There have been frequent rumors that single F-117 squadrons might be permanently based in the UK and Korea, but this seems unlikely. The aircraft has deployed to Europe, however, flying from British and Dutch air bases for exercises.

Having gone to war in the colors of the 37th TFW, the F-117A has also dropped bombs in anger while wearing the markings of its present unit, the 49th FW. Following the end of the Gulf War, Iraq became

bold in its violations of the ceasefire agreement, making incursions into Kuwait and across the boundaries of the no-fly zones imposed by the coalition allies. Allied aircraft patrolling these areas were threatened by Iraqi air defenses, and it became increasingly clear that Saddam Hussein would have to be taught another lesson. On 13 January 1993 six F-117As,

each carrying only a single bomb, attacked SAM sites, the SOC at Tallil and the IOC at Al Amara. None of the four aircraft attacking SAM sites hit their targets, thanks to broken laser locks, which were in turn caused by low cloud. The aircraft targeting the SOC at Tallil was unable even to find the target, but the remaining aircraft virtually destroyed the facility at Al Amara.

Above: The F-117A routinely uses a brake parachute to shorten its landing run. These are often black, like the rest of the aircraft. The chute bay is between the tailfins, which make its use impossible in a strong crosswind.

Left: The F-117A played vital role in the Gulf War, as the only allied warplane routinely assigned to attack targets in heavily-defended downtown Baghdad. Here a pilot waits to taxy at Khamis Mushayt, watched by his groundcrew. The F-117A is a unique shape in the sky, and improved computer power has allowed subsequent stealth aircraft to be designed with more curvaceous shapes.

FLYING CONTROLS

The F-117A's flying control surfaces consist of two elevons on the trailing edge of each wing, for pitch and roll control, while the all-moving tailfins (ruddervators) can move in unison to provide yaw control, or differentially to give pitch control. The control surfaces are actuated via the quadruplex GEC Astronics fly by wire control system.

weapons like JDAM actually have a lower accuracy than the F-117A's existing laser-guided bombs, while the aircraft remains relatively invulnerable to air defenses. More useful would be a new communications suite, with Low-Probability-of-Intercept (LPI) radio to allow pilots to talk to one another and to base, to allow changes in attack plans after takeoff.

In the longer term, it is still possible that the aircraft will undergo more drastic modifications. New electrochromic and thermalchromic coatings might be added to further reduce radar reflections and to

POWERPLANT

The F-117A is powered by a pair of 48-kN (10,800 lb st) General Electric F404-GE-F1D2 turbofans, unaugmented derivatives of the F404-GE-400 engines which power the F/A-18 Hornet. The F-117A is somewhat lacking in thrust, and many believe that the aircraft should be re-engined with a non-afterburning version of the F414, or even an afterburning engine, if the technical difficulties could be resolved.

suppress 75% of the aircraft's IR signature in the 3-5 and 8-12 micron ranges. Devices may be fitted to the engine exhausts to reduce visible exhaust glow, or alternatively, there have been proposals to fit afterburning engines, which would increase payload capability to up to 18,000 lb. Many pilots hope that a clear-view bubble canopy might be fitted (like that designed for the F-22, and for the naval F-117N/X. The USAF has always wanted the F-117 to carry a heavier weaponload, and this may eventually be

achieved, perhaps with a doubling of the internal load, and with some external weapons carriage for operations in low-threat areas. External weapons carriage no longer imposes quite the penalties that it once did, since low RCS pylons can be used in conjunction with radar-absorbent coatings on the weapons themselves. Proposals have also been made to incorporate a TARPS reconnaissance pod, which would presumably be lowered

FLYING THE F-117A

Improvements to the F-117's weapons system began in 1984, with the replacement of the aircraft's three F-16 type Delco M362F computers by three examples of the IBM Federal Systems/Loral AP-102 as used in the Space Shuttle, with an expanded data transfer module. Three computers are required because one is dedicated to the weapons delivery system, one to the navigation system, with the third serving as a back up. New composite bomb doors were fitted from much the same date. These improvements together conferred on the F-117A the ability to use two bombs (i.e. both bays) during a single pass, the aircraft having previously been restricted to single-bomb attacks. The ability to drop two bombs gave new capabilities: by dropping both on a single designated spot, the second bomb could punch through the hole blown by the first weapon, a useful trick when busting multi-layered bunkers.

Below: The F-117A is a simple and pleasant aircraft to fly, and pilots sneer at the continued use by the ill-informed of the 'Wobblin' Goblin' nickname applied early in the programme and now regarded as a historical curio. The aircraft's FBW control system gives it benign handling characteristics throughout the envelope.

At the time of the Gulf War, some F-117As still had their original metal bomb doors, but most had the new computer. By that time, the next phase of the improvement program was also well underway. This was known as OCIP (Offensive Capability Improvement Program) and the first modified aircraft made its first flight on 1 December 1988. The first 'production conversion' (805) was redelivered to Tonopah on 27 November 1990. The first seven OCIP-configured aircraft were ready and re-delivered, but were not deployed to Saudi Arabia for use in Desert Storm, remaining behind for training and other contingencies.

OCIP introduced a range of new features, including an improved FMS and autopilot (including autothrottle for the first time) and a number of cockpit improvements. The aircraft was given a new display processor, and the original monochrome display screens were replaced by Honeywell color MFDs, while a Harris Corporation Tactical Situation Display/digital moving map was also added, together with an LCD avionics function data-entry panel. Finally the aircraft incorporated a Pilot Activated Automatic Recovery System, which could return the aircraft to straight and level flight, established in a gentle climb, slightly nose-up, at the touch of a single button. Overall, the OCIP improvements improved pilot situational awareness and gave him more time to concentrate on his attack, requiring less effort, concentration and time to fly and navigate. The FMS improvements and autothrottle allowed the aircraft to fly more complex profiles automatically.

Redeliveries of OCIP-modified aircraft built up to a rate of one per month, and all had been modified by the end of 1995. In 1992, long before the basic OCIP program was complete, a third phase of improvements was flight tested. This involves replacement of the IRADS with new Texas Instruments FLIR and DLIR turrets, a Honeywell Ring Laser Gyro INS and a Collins GPS (Global Positioning System) using the stealthy antenna designed for the ATF (Advanced Tactical Fighter). The incorporation of GPS was prompted by combat experience in the Gulf, where extended five- or six-hour flights over the featureless desert gave little opportunity to update the existing INS. The new IRADS was fitted in an effort to double sensor and laser range, and reportedly allowed target acquisition and identification at 50% better ranges than were achieved during Operation Desert Storm, though exact figures are classified.

Further modifications are planned for the F-117A. Lockheed began work on a Mid Life Improvement Study (MIPS) during 1995. This was funded by the US Air Force and involves improvements to weapons, radar signature and other operational features. When further upgrades are commissioned, it is generally believed that they will almost certainly feature the incorporation of a MIL STD 1760 data bus. This would allow the aircraft's GPS to talk to the guidance systems of weapons like the JDAM or JSOW before launch, although the relevance of such stand-off weapons to the F-117A is not obvious at first sight. Certainly GPS-guided

FLYING TODAY'S MISSION:
PREPARING TO FLY

Proper operational briefings are not always so simple and straightforward as they were during training at Tonopah, since the F-117 may advantageously operate in conjunction with other aircraft types, and since unusual locations might require specialized intelligence briefings and updates. The aircraft can even make use of EF-111 Ravens for radar jamming, using jamming to mislead enemy forces as to the position and direction of the (invisible) attack force, or simply to replace delayed detection with no detection at all. In the USAF, the pilot will not necessarily plan his own mission, arriving at the squadron some hours after the officers designated as planners that day (a duty rotated among experienced F-117A pilots on a daily basis). In training at Tonopah and in the Gulf War alike, F-117A pilots tended to act as planners on one night and fly the next.

Tasking for the F-117A might come through normal channels in a conventional war, or might still come direct from the President, or from a specific special-operation joint-force commander. The tasking message will usually be very specific about the target and the required time on target, particularly since an F-117 strike might be carefully co-ordinated with action by special forces on the ground, or designed to open a corridor through enemy air defenses for conventional attack aircraft or bombers. The planners plan the required mission in detail, taking care to deconflict routeings and timings with other aircraft (the F-117A will be operating 'radio silent'). They will make use of a planning computer which remains one of the F-117A's most closely guarded secrets to this day. This incorporates a digital map of known air-defense radars, with their effective ranges against the Black Jet. This computer allows mission tapes to be prepared, which then allow the F-117A to evade enemy radars automatically.

Since the F-117A pilot does not plan his own mission, the briefing is particularly important, and covers the exact routeing as well as the attack itself. The briefing is an opportunity for the pilot to receive the very latest target information and intelligence, together with anticipated meteological conditions and all the usual details, from emergency procedures, alternate targets,

Left: Stealth Fighter pilots wear the same flying equipment and flight safety gear as all other USAF fast jet pilots.

Above: The pilot's signature indicates his formal assumption of responsibility for the aircraft he is about to fly.

diversion airfields, radio frequencies and air-defense corridors. Exact aim points are discussed and decided before flight, such points being far more specific than are routinely given to the pilots of other bombers. The ability of the Black Jet to hit not just a building, but a specific window, vent or room within that building, makes it necessary to target the most important part of a building. There is no point in taking out the store rooms if you can destroy the Minister's own office!

The accuracy of the F-117A's weapons system actually allows a more subtle approach to the 'blunt instrument' method of tactical bombing. If F-16s were assigned to knock out an electrical plant, several aircraft would be sent, attacking the major buildings as best they could, using sheer weight of numbers to destroy the sturdy generator room and the vulnerable but easy to repair water plant. By contrast a single F-117 might be assigned to knock out the plant's generator, which is critical, difficult to repair and easy to find.

After briefing, the pilot picks up his flying equipment, donning external anti-g trousers and a slimline back-type parachute. For an operational mission he will 'sanitize', emptying his pockets of anything personal, and of objects which might conceivably be of use to an enemy, from Movie theatre tickets to drugstore receipts. Finally he will strip the Velcro-backed patches from his flying suit and flight jacket. He will then put on his helmet and mask, connecting the intercom lead and oxygen hose to portable test equipment in the flight safety equipment room. On an operational mission, the pilot will also wear a survival vest, containing an escape kit, emergency rations and water, a survival knife, a 'Goolie chit' (or 'blood chit') in the appropriate language, offering a reward for his safe return and money in appropriate denominations for bribes during escape and evasion. The pilot will also carry a side arm, usually a 9-mm Beretta Model 92F automatic pistol. Perhaps most importantly, the pilot will carry a lightweight Motorola survival radio and transponder. The last task is to sign out the aircraft he has been assigned, carefully checking its modification state. Early in the Senior Trend program, it made a difference which aircraft you flew because each was built to a slightly different standard, with Lockheed incorporating improvements on the production line as they arose. Later in the life of the F-117A, various modification programs were incorporated by retrofit, and it took a great deal of time for these to become standard across the entire operational fleet.

Left: Checking the latest Met (weather) and any navigation warnings is a crucial step prior to going out to fly the mission. The F-117A's weapons and targeting sensors are extremely weather dependant.

Below: Before walking (or being driven) to the aircraft, the pilot checks the oxygen connectors and intercom leads of his flying helmet.

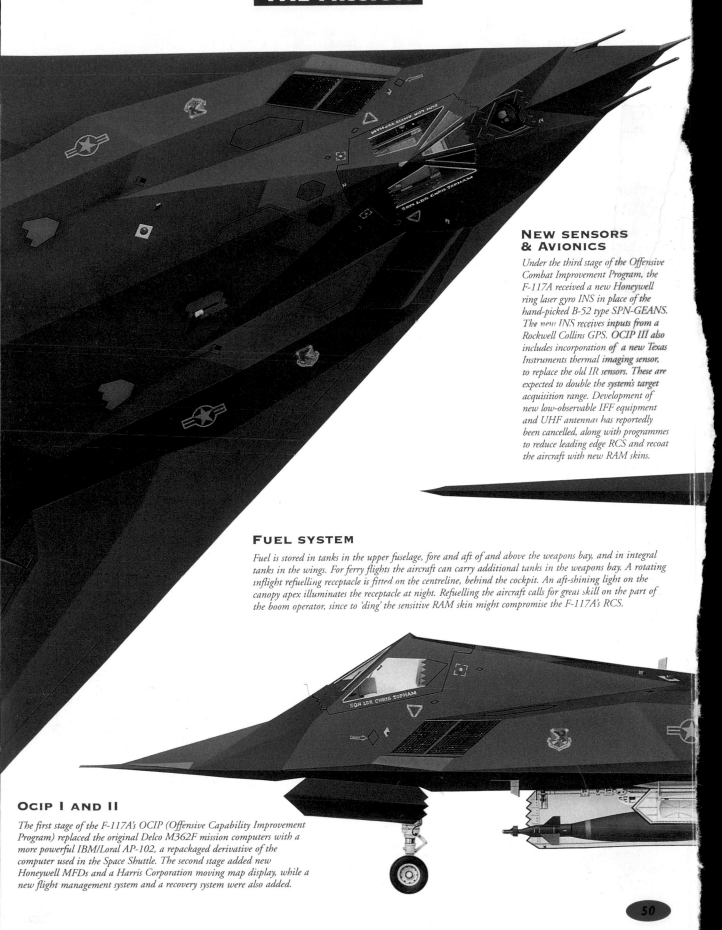

NEW SENSORS & AVIONICS

Under the third stage of the Offensive Combat Improvement Program, the F-117A received a new Honeywell ring laser gyro INS in place of the hand-picked B-52 type SPN-GEANS. The new INS receives inputs from a Rockwell Collins GPS. OCIP III also includes incorporation of a new Texas Instruments thermal imaging sensor, to replace the old IR sensors. These are expected to double the system's target acquisition range. Development of new low-observable IFF equipment and UHF antennas has reportedly been cancelled, along with programmes to reduce leading edge RCS and recoat the aircraft with new RAM skins.

FUEL SYSTEM

Fuel is stored in tanks in the upper fuselage, fore and aft of and above the weapons bay, and in integral tanks in the wings. For ferry flights the aircraft can carry additional tanks in the weapons bay. A rotating inflight refuelling receptacle is fitted on the centreline, behind the cockpit. An aft-shining light on the canopy apex illuminates the receptacle at night. Refuelling the aircraft calls for great skill on the part of the boom operator, since to 'ding' the sensitive RAM skin might compromise the F-117A's RCS.

OCIP I AND II

The first stage of the F-117A's OCIP (Offensive Capability Improvement Program) replaced the original Delco M362F mission computers with a more powerful IBM/Loral AP-102, a repackaged derivative of the computer used in the Space Shuttle. The second stage added new Honeywell MFDs and a Harris Corporation moving map display, while a new flight management system and a recovery system were also added.

on the trapeze for use. To further increase the aircraft's versatility, an LPI radar like that developed for the stillborn General Dynamics A-12 could be added, and this could confer a limited air-to-air capability, using the AIM-120 AMRAAM and the AIM-9X Sidewinder.

Having ascertained the exact standard of the aircraft assigned for the flight, the pilot will be driven to the aircraft's hangar or flightline. Here he talks to the crew chief. The airplane he is about to fly is very much the crew chief's baby, and this NCO will be intimately aware of exactly what the aircraft's individual servicing history has been, and what individual characteristics this particular airframe has. Having been built virtually by hand, at a very low rate, the F-117As were far from being uniform and they did have a degree of

individuality. Some were prone to particular faults and problems, while different aircraft had slightly different features and equipment. A crew chief works on only one aircraft, and his name (and the names of his team) are painted prominently on the aircraft's nosewheel door. Aircraft might also have a pilot's name on the canopy rail, but this was more symbolic, and a pilot would expect to fly whatever aircraft was available, perhaps never actually flying the aircraft with his name on it! A quick check of the aircraft's documentation completes the formal and official preparations, and the pilot signs to indicate his acceptance of the aircraft, in its current condition. This is vital, and cannot be skipped. Knowledge of recent defects and how they have been rectified may give the pilot a useful clue if something goes wrong on this flight. Moreover, some defects may be so minor that their repair or rectification might be deemed to have no impact on the aircraft's ability to fulfil its mission, and a repair can be deferred. The pilot needs to be aware of all such defects. With his signature he indicates that he is aware of all these factors, and that he is accepting the aircraft as being fit for flight. From now on, several million dollars' worth of F-117A is in

INDIVIDUAL AIRCRAFT HISTORY

This aircraft was later flown by Squadron Leader Chris Topham, the RAF's F-117A exchange pilot during the period 1990-1992. Topham's predecessor left the 37th just before the Gulf War, and Topham was still training when Desert Storm ended. Here the aircraft wears post-war markings, with high-visibility white 37th Fighter Wing and Holloman tailcodes, and with the Air Combat Command shield insignia high on the fins.

ARMAMENT

This aircraft carries a GBU-10 in the port weapons bay (seen here on the extended trapeze), with a GBU-27 in the other bay. This is a routine F-117A warload. Other weapons believed to be compatible with the F-117A include the AGM-88 HARM anti-radar missile, and the laser-guided AGM-114 Hellfire and AGM-65 Maverick. The bomb bay is relatively confined, and cannot accomodate the standard Paveway III (GBU-24) the GBU-27 being purpose built for the F-117A with the smaller tail unit of the Paveway II.

PRE-FLIGHT INSPECTION

Accompanying a pilot as he walked to his aircraft, and then as he conducted his walk-around inspection would be an excellent introduction to the unique features of the aircraft.

Right: The pre-flight walkaround is a vital part of every mission. There is no point at all in getting airborne in an aircraft which will not be able to fly the mission. Here a pilot checks his practice bombs.

THE BLACK JET

On seeing the F-117 sitting in its hangar or on the ramp, the first thing one might notice would be the aircraft's sinister, slightly sooty matt-black finish, which is reminiscent of the finish applied to U-2 and SR-71 spyplanes. Whether the aircraft needed to be black is open to some question. Certainly the special radar-absorbent paint used could be produced in other shades, while gray can be a better camouflage at night than black, (as demonstrated by German night fighters, during World War II) and gray is inevitably superior during daylight hours. Black is probably a very poor camouflage color,

especially if the finish is matt. The British Royal Air Force is currently painting its trainer aircraft glossy black overall to improve their conspicuity, and rejected matt-black paint only because it was more time-consuming to keep clean and smart! With its black paint the F-117A is hardly optically stealthy, except during the darkest nights. But succeeding generations of aircraft produced by Lockheed's Skunk Works have been painted black, and tradition (if nothing else) demanded that the Stealth fighter should have a similarly sinister paint job! The first YF-117A prototype was actually finished in a

INSIDE THE F-117A

The structure of the F-117A is entirely conventional, with a skeleton of ribs and stringers, spars and longerons. The faceted panels which form the skin are then attached to this structure. These panels are mostly aluminium, but are coated with RAM, applied in a sophisticated and automated 'spraybooth'.

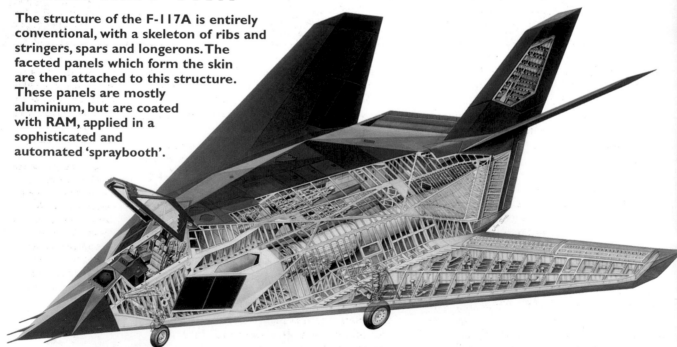

gray, with large patches of pale blue and red-brown added for the first few flights to hide its faceted shape. But General William Creech, the commanding general of the then Tactical Air Command, had definite ideas on what color 'his' new night bombers should be, and the order went out that all F-117As should be black, reportedly because he felt that this would best camouflage their faceted shape. It is possible to reduce an aircraft's conspicuity by using particular shades of paint, or by lighting certain areas to 'fill out' shadows, but this has not been attempted on the F-117A.

As an observant pilot approaches the F-117A, he might notice that other Stealth Fighters being prepared for flight do not have a host of open access panels, nor would he normally see groundcrew standing atop the aircraft, except when wearing specially designed cloth overboots. This is because the aircraft has been designed to have all sub-systems servicing access within the undercarriage and weapons bays, minimizing the number of frequently opened 'holes' in the aircraft's sensitive RAM-covered skin. There are other access panels for second-line servicing, but if these are opened, they have to be resealed, and the aircraft has to be re-painted in the area of the panel. No normal access panels are located on top of the aircraft, and there is a strict prohibition on anyone walking atop the wing or fuselage without the protective cloth overboots. The special paint which helps to give the aircraft its very low radar cross section is extremely vulnerable to damage, and is very highly classified. The unauthorized and uninitiated are still not even allowed to touch the aircraft's surface!

Above: This F-117A is seen in one of the Phase III shelters at Tonopah. The design of the hangars (known as Canyons) changed appreciably during the course of Tonopah's construction, and there are at least three distinct designs. All open at both ends, allowing the aircraft to taxy in, shut down, and be ready to taxy out without being turned. 'Old Glory' hangs in many of the shelters.

THE RADAR RIDDLE

Work on reducing radar cross section through the use of unusual skin materials is almost as old as radar itself, dating back to the war years. As early as 1943, the Horten brothers proposed using a sandwich skin, with granulated charcoal and sawdust as the center layer, whose sole purpose was to absorb radar energy. Serious efforts to reduce frontal RCS began in earnest during the 1950s, with the development of aluminium or iron-rich rubber coatings designed to absorb radar energy. Such material (known as RAM, or Radar Absorbent Material) was applied to a number of test-bed aircraft, and even in Britain RAM was applied to the leading edges of a Canberra bomber for trials. But while this gave useful results, it was clear that more could be achieved, especially if an aircraft were to be designed with a low radar cross section (low-observability) as a primary requirement.

Above: The observer cannot tell what ordnance load is being carried by an F-117A, since everything is carried in the fore-and-aft split weapons bay. Beyond confirming the use of the GBU-27 Paveway III and GBU-10 Paveway II in the Gulf, the USAF is coy about what weapons can be carried, stating merely that it is compatible with all air-to-ground weapons in the inventory. This is inaccurate, since many weapons will not fit in the narrow and short confines of the F-117A's bomb bay.

The use of surface coatings to reduce radar cross section was explored more thoroughly on the Lockheed SR-71 Blackbird and the U-2, which were painted with a paint containing carbonyl iron ferrites, and known as 'iron ball' paint. When a radar wave hit the paint, it induced a magnetic field within the metallic elements of the paint, the field switching polarity and dissipating the electrical energy of the radar pulse, rather than reflecting the energy back. Much of the radar's energy is actually transformed into heat. As well as radar-absorbent paint, radar-absorbent material (RAM) can be manufactured in neoprene-like tiles, which incorporate similar active ferric compounds in the synthetic polymer matrix.

The effectiveness of the F-117A's RAM skin was demonstrated in an unusual manner during the Gulf War, when groundcrews started finding dead bats around the tails of the hangared aircraft. The unfortunate creatures had clearly flown "full tilt" into the Black Jet's tailfins, which their high frequency 'sonar' had been unable to detect.

The F-117A made extensive use of RAM in sheet form (similar to lino in thickness and composition, but significantly heavier), with thicknesses differing on different parts of the airframe. These sheets were metal-backed, and were cut to shape, then bonded directly to the aircraft's metal skin or substructure. Gaps between the sheets were sealed with RAM applied in paint or putty form, while some panels would be sealed only during operations, using tape or paint. RAM paint is difficult to apply consistently to an accurate thickness, and requires the use of highly toxic solvents. Despite this, the F-117A now uses paint-type RAM instead of sheets, and this is applied using robotics. The paint facility at Holloman AFB uses a giant cradle to hold and move the aircraft, and computer-controlled paint nozzles.

The use of RAM alone would have given the F-117A a significantly reduced radar cross section, but would not have given the aircraft its present level of invisibility. Below the skin, some use is made of radar-absorbent structure, including what are known as re-entrant triangles, which tend to trap radar energy, bouncing it around from face to face internally, dissipating it instead of reflecting it back. A similar structure was pioneered in the SR-71.

But the key to the success of the Stealth Fighter's stealthiness lies in the solution of a mathematician's riddle. Radar works by measuring the energy reflected back by a target. If a target can absorb some of the energy it will reduce the effective range of the radar and help to confuse those trying to analyze radar returns. A second way to 'spoil' radar is to reflect energy away from the transmitter, giving it no returns to measure. The crucial breakthrough in producing a Stealth aircraft came with the rediscovery of formulae which allowed an accurate prediction of the reflection of Electro-Magnetic Radiation (e.g. radar energy) from a two-dimensional object. The basic formulae for predicting the radar reflectivity of a geometric object were worked out early this century by James Clark Maxwell (a Scot) and were refined by the German Arnold Johannes. These formulae were rediscovered by the Soviet scientist Pyotr Ufimtsev, who applied the formulae to predict the RCS of a particular two dimensional object. His paper was published in 1966, winning its author a prestigious State Prize. Fortunately, no-one tried to apply his theories in the USSR. A

Lockheed Skunk works mathematician, Denys Overholser discovered Ufimtsev's paper and created a software program ('Echo 1') which could work out the RCS of an aircraft composed of flat panels, but not of a conventional rounded aircraft. From the software program it was a short step to design the optimum shape for minimizing RCS, the so-called 'Hopeless Diamond', on which the F-117A is closely based.

Thus the solution of a mathematical problem accounts for the Black Jet's angular shape, with the external surface made up entirely of sharp-edged flat panels set at angles to one another. No attempt has been made to round off corners or to add curves, the shape is quite clearly made up of hundreds of faceted plates.

Beneath the surface outline, the aircraft is less radical than its shape might suggest. Perhaps mindful of its early unflattering cockroach nickname, Lockheed described the 'central carapace' as having a skeleton of ribs and stringers, with larger structural members running through the key load routes, and to which was attached a shell of faceted panels. The wings are built around a two-spar box, and are attached to the fuselage by five main bolts along the inter-spar interface with three more bolts forward of the front spar, and with an angled strut attaching the rear spar to the fuselage immediately forward of the exhaust.

With a production run of less than 60 aircraft, unit cost of the F-117A was inevitably going to be high, but sensible economies were made to keep the price down to an astonishingly low figure. Wherever possible, existing equipment and systems were used, saving the cost of developing, testing and proving new items. Use of parts from other aircraft types also had a security advantage. No-one would notice an order for extra F404 engines (used by the F/A-18) or for additional F-16 flight-control-system computers and actuators. Thus while the F-117's unique shape makes it look 'all new' it in fact makes extensive use of existing technology, equipment and parts. Approaching the aircraft from the rear, no-one could guess that the long, flat exhaust slots served the familiar F404 engine, though there are other, more obvious clues to the type's reliance on existing aircraft 'parts bins'. The undercarriage, for example, is made by Menasco, but uses a nose oleo which comes from an A-10A, while the wheels are from the F-16. The ECS was a standard Hercules item, and the Sundstrand APU turbine starter came from the F/A-18.

By the time the pilot arrives at his aircraft, if it is a pre-OCIP machine, it will have been connected to external power for some time, to allow the INS to be fully aligned. This process takes about 43 minutes under normal circumstances. The INS is an old-fashioned piece of equipment, and is actually the Honeywell SPN-JEANS navigation system as used by the Boeing B-52. This helps to explain the extended alignment time required, but not the extraordinary accuracy and minimal drift rate of the equipment (the drift rate is claimed as better than 0.12 nm per hour, which is less than 128 yards, or 384 feet, after flying more than 400 miles). The

INS had an electrostatic gimbal, with gyros housed in a metal sphere, this being suspended in a magnetic field. INS units in the F-117As were hand-picked and specially calibrated, and are thus even more reliable and precise than those fitted to Boeing B-52s. Today, the increasing cost of supporting the out-of-production INS is high, and the unit is being replaced by a ring laser gyro INS and a GPS. The pilot can take off with a partially aligned INS if necessary, but accuracy and drift-rate figures are considerably worse than for a fully aligned INS.

Before conducting his walk-around inspection of the aircraft, the pilot checks certain switch positions in the cockpit. The walk-around inspection should be unnecessary, since the groundcrew will already have given the aircraft a thorough daily inspection. Nevertheless, the pilot has signed for the aircraft and he will follow the usual ritual, circling slowly round the aircraft and visually inspecting the control surfaces,

Above: Reports suggest that the F-117A has recently assumed a defence suppression role, hunting mobile SAMs using the AGM-88 HARM missile. It is unclear how the F-117 detects and locates enemy SAM radars, but may rely on third-party targeting by F-16s, with which it has recently exercised in the Wild Weasel role.

tyres, and a host of other details. He will check the sit of the aircraft, and that there are no untoward leaks. Above all, he will carefully check the condition of the RAM skin.

The F-117A's unusual and unconventional configuration meant that the aircraft could not be made aerodynamically stable, in the conventional sense, and that the aircraft could not be 'flown' without the aid of sophisticated stability augmentation in the form of a modern digital fly-by-wire control system. Without such a system, the aircraft suffered from severe pitch instability and moderate directional instability. Only a computer could react quickly enough to keep

Above: The USAF's small but vital fleet of F-117As have received a succession of modification programmes. These have transformed the aircraft's capabilities, without altering its external appearance at all.

the aircraft from diverging from straight and level flight, and the computerized flight-control system thus acts as an interface between the human pilot and the aircraft's control surfaces. The pilot makes a control input, and the computer then ensures that the aircraft maneuvers in accordance with that input, while preventing the aircraft from tumbling out of control. Trying to fly an inherently unstable aircraft has been likened to attempting to steer a bicycle backwards, by its handlebars, while sitting on the front of a speeding car, pushing the bike along at 70 miles an hour. A sophisticated computer could make tiny corrections quickly enough to keep the bicycle straight, but a human would find the bike's handlebars torn from his hands within seconds. The aircraft was therefore fitted with a re-programmed and modified version of the FCS used in the General Dynamics F-16.

At the point of the aircraft's nose, there are four short faceted probes. As a quadruplex system, the Lear Siegler Astronics fly-by-wire Flight Control System required four separate sources of air data. Ideally air data would

have been provided via static ports flush with the aircraft's skin, but it proved impossible to find four suitable locations for separate sensors for yaw, pitch, AoA, q (dynamic pressure) and airspeed where the airflow did not make the variables affect each other. Therefore, the decision was made to employ four separate pitot probes, though these were to prove one of the most severe headaches encountered by the designers. It was difficult to design a faceted probe which could gather the necessary information, but conventional pitch and yaw vanes were clearly out of the question. As built, each pitot probe had a pyramid-shaped tip, with a flattened point containing one aperture, and with four more apertures on each 'facet'. The tips of the probes are the only part of the F-117A which are not coated with RAM, and are said to be responsible for a very high proportion of the aircraft's RCS. Providing heat to prevent the probes from icing up proved to be an almost intractable problem, and initially the F-117A was prohibited from flying in icing conditions or in cloud. Eventually, a very fine non-conductive heating filament was designed, this being the thickness of a human hair, and thus having a negligible affect on radar cross section. This took two and a half years!

Looking up the nose from the probes, the pilot can see the FLIR turret behind a fine wire-mesh screen. The FLIR is one of two identical and interchangeable turret-mounted sensors (the other being the DLIR, mounted below the nose, offset to starboard), differing only in calibration and alignment. The DLIR image is inverted electronically for 'natural sense' display in the cockpit. The turrets are modified versions of the FLIR used by the Rockwell OV-10D Bronco, linked to an enlarged servo controller and video tracker. On the ground, the FLIR turret will be rotated to face aft, so its distinctive three windows are not visible. They serve the narrow and wide field of view FLIR modes, and the laser designator.

The IRADS turrets are housed behind simple wire-mesh screens, which allow the passage of a broad spectrum of IR and laser energy, but which reflect radar energy. The screen uses copper wires which provide electrical continuity across the bay, and each one costs $7,000. This may seem expensive for a piece of wire mesh, but the alternative would have been a screen made of Gallium Arsenide or Germanium, which would have been $500,000! The leading edge of the 'frame' containing the mesh had a saw tooth, designed to reflect radar energy in different directions. Most edges aligned with the likely direction of enemy radar waves were similarly 'jagged', including the front and rear edges of the bomb bay doors, the canopy side windows, and the nosewheel door.

Cavities and apertures in the RAM-covered skin are avoided at all costs, so, like the IRADS turrets, the engine intakes have to be covered by grids which appear as solid facets to radar, while still allowing air to enter without distortion. The grids covering the engine intakes are constructed from elements which are themselves faceted in cross-section and coated with RAM. Most radar energy is absorbed in the skin of the grid, or reflected around within the grid. Very little radar energy reaches the compressor face of the engine, and even less returns through the grid. The intake grids have the advantage of acting as flow straighteners, but are prone to icing, acting like freezer ice trays, and requiring a unique fluid de-icing system. To ensure that the intakes are clear of ice, the pilot can switch on small lamps set into the cockpit sides, which shine back and illuminate the intake grids. Above the intakes are auxiliary suck-in doors, which open when greater mass flow is required, mainly on takeoff.

The F-117A has an arrow-like wing planform, with sharply swept wing leading edges. The notched Delta shape gave maximum sweep, yet also allowed maximum aspect ratio (the ratio of span to chord) which improved lift and drag characteristics. The high wing sweep angle was selected not to improve supersonic performance (the aircraft is very much a subsonic bomb truck) but to reflect radar waves away from their source instead of back to it. Remarkably, the production F-117A actually has reduced sweep by comparison with the original XST concept demonstrator. This gave higher lift, without materially reducing the effectiveness of the wing planform in reflecting away radar waves. The leading edges themselves are extremely sharp, to maximize low observability, though this was not ideal for a subsonic airfoil. The wings were made detachable to make rapid deployment of partially disassembled aircraft (aboard C-5 Galaxies) more easy.

It was decided that a conventional horizontal tail would impose an unacceptable RCS penalty, and this necessitated the provision of full-span, four-section elevons for pitch and roll control. They could not be drooped as flaps, and leading-edge high-lift devices were judged to be impractical. The control surfaces were sealed with flexible

Above: All apertures in the F-117A's skin are covered, sealed with RAM putty, or covered by radar-reflecting and absorbing screens. The IRADS turrets lie behind a fine wire mesh, while cruder screens cover the engine intakes.

RAM, with no appreciable gap between the wing itself and the flaps.

The engine exhausts were made by ASTECH/MI and tapered from the standard circular section to a broad, flat slot, five feet wide, but only four inches deep. The broad, flat louvres were manufactured from nickel alloy 718 honeycomb sandwich to cope with heat and pressure. They incorporate baffles to keep the flow straight, with other baffles and plates to break up radar waves, and to block any view of the hot exhaust of the engine. Bypass air cools the surrounding structure and the exhaust plume itself, while heat-reflective tiles protect the most vulnerable parts of the structure. The wide, flat exhaust plume cools very quickly, making the aircraft less vulnerable to detection by IR-based sensors.

Tailfins were selected for yaw control, instead of split elevon tips, which would have had less control authority and which would have generated greater drag. The tailfins were always going to be canted, since a vertical fin would inevitably reflect radar waves straight back at their source. The XST's inward canted fins had been designed to shield the engine exhausts from above, which they did, though they also hindered dissipation of the hot exhaust gases, making the aircraft more visible to IR sensors. The production aircraft would have had its fins far too far apart if they had been mounted outboard of the platypus exhausts, whether canted inboard or outboard. Instead, an outward canted V tail was mounted on an extension to the fuselage spine.

INTERNAL WEAPONS BAY

Ducking under the broad, not quite flat belly, the pilot checks inside the undercarriage bays, and inside the bomb bay. It was clear from the start that the F-117A would carry its weapons internally, since external carriage would have made a low RCS impossible to obtain. This necessitated the provision of a large internal weapons bay, and this drove the size of the aircraft. The F-117A's weapons bay is located between the engines, with a unique hoist or trapeze provided for weapon loading and launching. The bay is actually divided into two, with separate doors hinged at the inboard edge, closest to the centerline. Each bay actually has a separate trapeze.

In use, the trapeze can swing down below the level of the aircraft's belly, giving the aircraft the theoretical capability of carrying rail-launched missiles like the AIM-9 Sidewinder or AGM-65 Maverick. Originally, all weapons had to be released from the lowered trapeze, with bombs dropping off under gravity, and not being ejected pyrotechnically. Small perforated baffles swung down in front of the trapezes to improve airflow for bomb release. Use of the trapeze in the lowered position is not favored, since it increases the time during which the doors are open, and radically increases the aircraft's radar cross section during this time. It has been calculated that use of the trapeze actually increases exposure time by about a factor of five. The trapeze now remains within the bay when freefall weapons are being dropped, making an LGB drop relatively quick, and exposing the aircraft to the risk of detection for a shorter time.

The weapons bay was sized to accommodate the GBU-10 Paveway II LGB, based on the 2,000 lb Mk 84 iron bomb. The weapon has a gimballed seeker, with full-deflection guidance, meaning that the control fins can move only to the neutral position or to full deflection. This means that the bomb bounces from one side of the 'basket' to the other, losing energy and momentum. When using a Paveway II-based weapon it is vital to lob it accurately into the center of the 'basket' (the cone of reflected laser energy reflected by the target) and to 'lase' (designate) the target late. This gives the minimum number of corrections to the bomb to prevent it porpoising down the basket, losing energy all the way. In the normal mode, the F-117A's computer shuts off the laser (which has up to now been providing range information) as the bomb is released, firing it again only seconds from impact. This ensures that the bomb hits at a better angle, with much greater momentum.

Ironically, sizing the bay for the GBU-10

made it too short to accommodate the basic Paveway III 2,000 lb bomb, which was being developed by Texas Instruments amid great secrecy at much the same time as the F-117A. The new bomb used a novel proportional guidance system, moving the control surfaces only as much as was necessary to make minor corrections to the course. This meant that the bomb 'flapped about' far less in the basket, retaining more energy. When it was finally unveiled, it became apparent that the GBU-24 Paveway III's long wings projected well beyond the tail when retracted, and a special derivative of the weapon was developed for carriage by the F-117, using the shorter 500 lb Mk 82-based Paveway II GBU-12 tail. The smaller tail restricted low-level toss-bombing performance, but this was never intended to be a feature of F-117A operations. With the new tail, the Mk 84-based Paveway III became the GBU-27B, while a similar weapon using the hard (4340 steel alloy)-cased, tail-fused BLU-109B penetrator became the GBU-27A/B. Even with the shorter tail, the GBU-27s are almost as long as the weapons bay itself and there were once fears that the bombs would have to be lowered on their trapezes before release. Fortunately, trials showed that the weapon could be dropped directly out of the bay, without lowering the trapeze. The GBU-27 can be dropped in two modes with pre-programmed impact angles, either following a ballistic trajectory against targets with some vertical extent, or pitching nose down to penetrate vertically.

It seems likely that the GBU-10 and GBU-27 are actually the only weapons routinely carried by the F-117A, although some other weapons have seen limited use, and yet others (probably including the nuclear B.61) have been cleared for use, but have not been deployed operationally. Some 27 500-lb GBU-12 Paveway IIs were used on a couple of occasions during the Gulf War, most notably against oil-filled trenches and pipelines in Kuwait. At one stage, the F-117A squadrons also wanted to use unguided CBUs against SAM sites, but the weapons were being used by A-10s and F-16s, and could not be transported to Khamis Mushayt. Unguided 2,000 lb bombs were also used by the F-117A for attacks on a large factory building for which intelligence could provide no specific aim point, and against which it would have been wasteful to use an expensive guidance kit! In the early days of

the program, the USAF's position was that the aircraft carried "the full range of tactical munitions in the inventory", but in recent years the statement has tended to be that the F-117A is compatible with "a full range" of such munitions. The USAF would certainly like to expand the range and weight of weapons carried by the F-117A, but the aircraft is severely limited by the size of its internal weapons bays.

During the pilot's walk-around inspection he will look up into the bay with great care, probably using a torch, and perhaps with his groundcrew holding more light sources. Inside the bay he checks the condition and correct attachment of various locking wires and fuse settings, and makes sure that the arming lanyards have been fitted properly.

Above: A GBU-10 Paveway II hangs down on the starboard trapeze (on the left of this picture) with the more modern GBU-27 Paveway III on the port trapeze.

INTO THE COCKPIT

Following the walk-around, the pilot again mounts the flimsy aluminium ladder to the cockpit, steps over the sill, and settles into the seat. Inevitably, he will be followed by one of the groundcrew, who will pass him the mountain of paperwork and equipment that he will require during the flight ahead. Despite the sophisticated navigation system, the pilot will take several maps on the mission, a large-scale one showing the IP-to-target run and the egress, and others showing the overall routeing and diversions, with timings, fuel states, and headings to fly, as well as headings to fly to the best diversion at each point of the mission. In a pre-OCIP aircraft the pilot would have had to refer to his maps, since his monochrome MFDs would have displayed only a graphic representation of the route, but in a post-OCIP aircraft the digital moving map should make his conventional paper maps more of a back-up. He will have target photos (taken by satellite, U-2 or intelligence assets in-country) and a checklist of operations for every stage of the flight, with comprehensive emergency procedures to deal with any crisis.

Below: Colonel Alton Whitley was the first TAC pilot to fly the F-117A, and as a Lt Col led the first frontline unit. He later led the 37th TFW to war in the Gulf, and is seen here on his return to Nellis AFB.

As the groundcrew remove the ladder and make ready for the pilot to taxi, he stows away all his kit (which might include an NBC suit and mask) and begins to go through the pre-flight checklist. For a typical operational flight, the initial checks take up to an hour, as the pilot exhaustively satisfies himself as to the correct operation of the aircraft's various systems. Probably the pilot's first action once the ladder has been removed from the cockpit rail is to insert the electronic memory cartridge (the EDTM, or Electronic Data Transmission Module) into the Data Transfer Unit. This loads the mission plan into the aircraft computer. If the EDTM fails to function, or if last-minute changes have to made, the pilot can input the data directly, using a key pad.

Although the F-117A is not renowned as being unreliable, the aircraft can be temperamental and is sometimes prone to ground aborts. If there is a spare aircraft, and if there is time, the pilot will unload his EDTM, grab his maps and photos and sprint to the spare aircraft and, exceptionally, might find himself getting as far as beginning the checklist in three different aircraft. It certainly is not unheard of. During the process, the pilot can communicate with the groundcrew, whose headsets are plugged into a socket in the nosewheel bay via a long umbilical. As the pilot runs through his checklist, the groundcrew have their own checks and procedures to follow. For a no-kidding

operational sortie, the bomb bay doors are sealed with metallic tape and are then 'buttered' with RAM putty or sprayed with RAM paint. The canopy may undergo similar treatment. The standing joke is that the final item on the pre-taxi checklist is to ensure that the RAM putty is properly dry! All RAM repairs are checked using a JOST gun, ensuring that the radar reflectiveness and absorption characteristics are uniform across old and new skin.

Like the aircraft itself, the cockpit of the F-117 was shaped by its genesis within the black world. Existing equipment was used wherever possible, since any new item might attract the unwelcome question, "What's it for?" Thus the cockpit does not represent the very cutting edge of man-machine interface technology and does not represent the state of the art. The main instrument panel is somewhat cluttered, with three large display screens; the central one is a TV dedicated to displaying imagery from the FLIR and DLIR, with slightly smaller multi-function displays to its left and right. These are surrounded by input buttons, allowing the pilot to call up a variety of displays and menus.

The rest of the panel includes a cluster of standby analogue flight instruments in the far left hand corner, armament and bomb door controls below the left hand MFD, a radalt, standby artificial horizon and slip ball below the right hand screen, and with a g-meter, engine and fuel instruments on the right hand side of the panel. Clusters of four warning annunciator lights are mounted at the apex of the instrument panel, on each side of the HUD. These are not the normal systems warnings found in other aircraft types though, they are warning lights which illuminate if the aircraft's low observability is compromised, and indicate the nature of the problem.

Pilots from some aircraft types might even find certain items in the cockpit familiar, and certainly few find adapting to the F-117 difficult. An F/A-18 Hornet pilot would feel immediately at home, since the stick-top, throttles, modified Kaiser AVQ-18 HUD and Texas Instruments multi-function display screens are standard F/A-18 items, together with the fuel controls. Although the HUD itself was from the F/A-18, the optics were from the Alpha Jet. The primary sensor display was developed for use in the OV-10D and P-3C, while the navigation system was taken from the B-52. The simplicity and familiarity of the cockpit helps to explain why there is no two-seat trainer version of the aircraft. There doesn't need to be. The

cockpit has few unique features, and any fast jet pilot worth his salt could probably master the Stealth Fighter by reading the flight manual and listening carefully to a good brief from an instructor. In fact, conversion to the aircraft is eased through use of a simulator, though the first pilots in the program converted to the airplane without this luxury.

Although the F-117A has undergone a fairly major upgrade, including modernization of the cockpit, this is not readily apparent until the displays are switched on. From a cursory glance, or even from the brief check of key items before the walk-around, the F-117A cockpit today looks much the same as it has always been.

If the F-117 were being built today, it would almost certainly have a more conventional-looking cockpit canopy, giving the pilot a better view of the outside world. But at the time it was built, the F-117 needed a canopy that was as faceted as the aircraft itself, and this required a strong backbone structure. Furthermore, it proved impossible to give transparent materials the same radar absorption and reflectivity characteristics as solid materials, even though they were thinly coated with gold, so they were limited in size and area. The five transparencies in the canopy and windscreen were manufactured

Above: The F-117A's cockpit has been modernised and upgraded, and this photo shows the pre-OCIP configuration. Two CRT MFDs flank the central IRADS display screen, on which an IR picture is displayed in eerie green monochrome. The pilot carries checklists and target photos on his kneeboards.

by the Sierracin/Sylmar Corporation. Thus the F-117 has a more heavily framed canopy than any other tactical aircraft in the inventory, and when it is closed, the cockpit seems darker, more claustrophobic, and offers poorer visibility than anything the average fighter pilot has experienced. The pilot has no view of his rear hemisphere, and the view down over the nose and to the sides is poor. Keeping track of an opponent in an air-to-air close-in dogfight would be virtually impossible in this 'fighter'.

But in keeping with US practice and tradition, the F-117's cockpit is at least large and spacious, a far cry from the cramped (loyal pilots call them snug!) quarters in some European fighters. And the cockpit is comfortable. The F-117 cockpit has clearly benefited from the input of pilots themselves and from some high-powered human-factors and ergonomics specialists. The aircraft is comfortable to fly for extended periods, allowing long-range and high-endurance operations without unacceptable degradation of pilot performance. Short of installing two seats, a crew rest bunk, a toilet and a galley (all features of the latest Russian 'tactical' aircraft, the Sukhoi Su-27IB) the aircraft could not be better for long flights.

The ejection seat is a standard McDonnell Douglas ACES II seat, re-painted in certain areas to reduce 'glint', but otherwise unchanged. The seat is rocket-powered for smooth acceleration (reducing the likelihood of back injuries) and is capable of operation at zero height and zero forward speed. But, more than in other tactical aircraft, the F-117 pilot is aware that the seat is only one link in his 'escape system'. When sitting under acres of clear perspex, pilots realize that, in extremis, they could probably eject through the canopy if it failed to jettison, or if the embedded detonator cord failed to explode the canopy into powder and fragments. Many seats even have sharp steel spikes in their head fairings for just this eventuality. But the heavy steel structure of the F-117 canopy makes it immediately apparent that ejection would be impossible unless the canopy was jettisoned first. Checking that the safety pins for canopy jettison have been removed may thus have just a touch more significance to the F-117 pilot.

Once strapped in, the pilot reaches forward and pulls back the elephant ears (large hinged anti-glare shields), which are stowed atop the instrument panel coaming. These shield the instruments and screens from light outside the cockpit (preventing distracting reflections),

F-117A COCKPIT LAYOUT

Noteworthy features of the F-117A cockpit included 'eyebrow' RCS warning lights along the edges of the cockpit coaming, in a position calculated to make them ideal 'attention-getters'. All engine parameters are displayed digitally, below and to the right of the starboard CRT screen. The cockpit shown is typical of an OCIP I aircraft.

HOTAS

The designers clustered all vital controls on the throttle and control column, allowing the pilot to make all necessary routine switch selections without taking his hands off the flying controls. This is known as HOTAS (Hands-On-Throttle-And-Stick). The controls on the throttles included a full freedom of movement thumb rocker which the pilot used to move the IRADS turret over the target. Depressing the switch generated the solid box used to obtain a contrast lock. Rotary rockers on the front of the throttle were used to adjust image level and gain, while a 'Pinkie' switch on the outer face of the throttles dimmed all cockpit lighting. The throttle also accomodated the black hot/white hot selector and the radio transmit switch.

and hide the F-117's own instrument glow outside the cockpit. Starting the engines is simple, and is achieved by using the built-in APU. The engines are non-afterburning General Electric F404-GE-F1D2 turbofans, each rated at approximately 48 kN (10,800 lb st). These were derived from the engines used by the F/A-18 Hornet, and had a three-stage fan, with a bypass ratio of 0.34. The relatively low bypass ratio minimizes mass flow, thus minimizing the size, volume and weight of the engine intakes and intake ducts. From the fan, the airflow passes through a seven-stage high pressure compressor, an annular combustion chamber, and single-stage high and low pressure turbines.

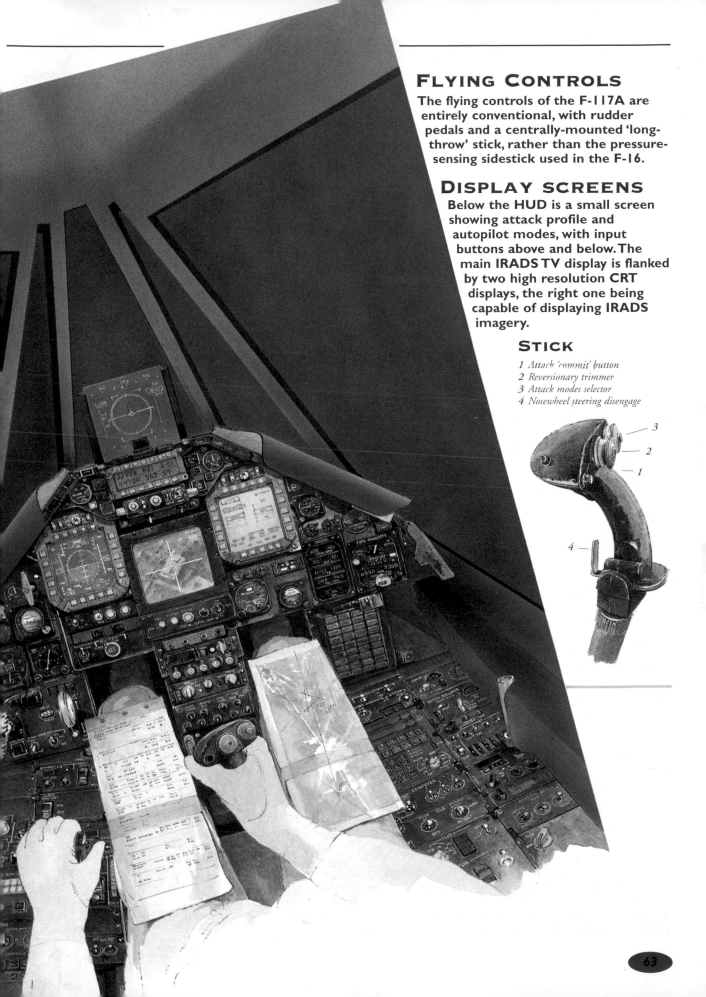

FLYING CONTROLS

The flying controls of the F-117A are entirely conventional, with rudder pedals and a centrally-mounted 'long-throw' stick, rather than the pressure-sensing sidestick used in the F-16.

DISPLAY SCREENS

Below the **HUD** is a small screen showing attack profile and autopilot modes, with input buttons above and below. The main **IRADS** TV display is flanked by two high resolution **CRT** displays, the right one being capable of displaying **IRADS** imagery.

STICK

1 Attack 'commit' button
2 Reversionary trimmer
3 Attack modes selector
4 Nosewheel steering disengage

RADIO SILENT TAKE OFF

At Tonopah, the aircraft inevitably taxied out in darkness, usually without any external lights. A FLIR picture could be displayed in the HUD, but NVGs (Night Vision Goggles), which would have been useful for looking out of the aircraft outside the FLIR's gimbal limits, were not used. The aircraft were guided by groundcrew with torches or glowing 'wands'. The aircraft would usually taxi out with its nose oleo mounted taxi-light on, and with wingtip navigation lights glowing. The flashing red anti-collision beacon is a peacetime only option, however, since it is scabbed on externally, increasing RCS.

The entire mission may be radio silent, from start-up to shut-down, though usually there are brief routine reports to be made at specific points during the mission. Training flights are made under the same procedures as are used by other tactical aircraft, and during the Black years at Tonopah the aircraft were operated under the guise of being A-7s.

The F-117A is an easy aircraft to taxi, with a

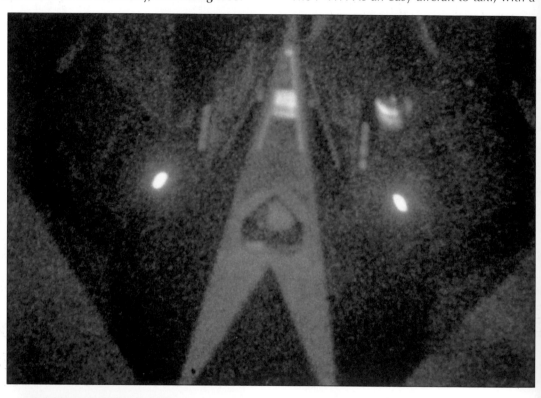

Right: An F-117A en route to Baghdad, as seen by the boomer of a KC-135 tanker. The glowing green dots on each side of the cockpit are the lights which allow the pilot to check that his intakes are not icing up.

Below: The F-117A cockpit, pre-OCIP. The cockpit is strongly reminiscent of that of the F/A-18, and uses some of the same instruments. It is dominated by the unique IRADS display, flanked by a pair of CRT multi-function displays. The stick top is basically that of the F/A-18, albeit with different switches and buttons to suit the Stealth Fighters' unique role.

good turning radius on the ground, and with reasonable visibility on the ground. The pilot can use the boresighted FLIR to taxi accurately even in total darkness. Reaching the holding point, the F-117A pilot conducts his final pre-takeoff checks and then taxies onto the runway as briefed. He might do this at a pre-briefed time, or on receiving a visual signal from the tower, or from a runway caravan. With no flaps and no afterburner, the aircraft accelerates slowly and uses a lot of runway before it reaches unstick speed (180 kt, 207 mph). The F-117A's engines are relatively widely spaced, although the broad flat exhausts minimize thrust asymmetry in the event of an engine failure. If an engine does fail after takeoff, the pilot will already have reached single-engined safety speed, and the aircraft can easily be held straight using rudder. The rudder pedals are actually disabled when the gear is retracted, and an automatic yaw trimmer takes over. In most cases, the correct drill following an engine failure is to retract the landing gear and maintain AoA and bank angle, letting the aircraft keep itself straight using the yaw trimmer.

Airborne, the pilot retracts the landing gear, moving his left hand briefly from the throttles to the chunky up/down selector at the base of

pleasant working environment, slightly noisier than that of the A-10, but considerably quieter than the cockpits of aircraft like the F-4, F-15 and Jaguar.

Shortly after takeoff, the Stealth pilot normally makes a radio check. First he reaches down with his right hand and flips the toggle switch for the RLS from 'RETRACT' through 'AUTO' to 'EXTEND'. This extends a

the right hand side of the main panel, watching for the three green lights to extinguish, confirming that the gear is up and locked. The hiss of bleed air increases, just slightly, as the gear doors close fully, while there is a dull thump as the blow-in auxiliary intake doors shut. With the gear up, the aircraft's RCS is suddenly minuscule, and if navigation lights were used on the ground, they are now turned off and will remain off (except perhaps during in-flight refuelling) until the aircraft is back in the circuit, preparing to land. Once in cruising flight, the pilot will check fuel flow and contents. Fuel is the preoccupation of every military pilot, since missions are inevitably tightly planned with regard to payload/fuel/range considerations. The F-117A has an internal fuel capacity of some 12,000 lb, and in normal flight, fuel flow is about 3,000 lb per hour. The F-117A cockpit is a relatively

tiny retractable blade antenna above the fuselage spine, offset slightly to starboard. This tiny antenna dramatically affects the aircraft's radar cross section, so has to be retractable, and is extended only briefly and only in friendly airspace. The 'AUTO' position would extend the antenna automatically when the pilot thumbed his radio transmit switch, but if he did this inadvertently over hostile territory the consequences could be serious, so he would most likely check and retract the antenna, leaving the switch in retract, with the power switch next to it in the 'OFF' position. He will extend the antenna only when expecting a pre-briefed message, perhaps a Go-No Go codeword. During the black years at Tonopah, antennas would be left extended for the duration of the mission, and the pilot would make routine radio calls as though he were flying a LANA-equipped A-7 - the F-117A's 'cover'.

Above: F-117As en route to the target. Pictured from a tanker is an F-117A waiting for his wingman to finish refuelling. In the background, another F-117A approaches another KC-10 tanker.

INSTRUMENT FLYING

Above: The F-117A's autopilot is linked to the INS and mission computer and is programmed to make turns which minimise exposure to hostile radar.

The F-117A's sophisticated quadruplex fly-by-wire control system makes it a simple, easy aircraft to fly, although on a typical operational mission, the F-117A pilot actually does little real 'piloting', leaving most of the flight in the capable hands of the aircraft's highly sophisticated autopilot. This can fly the entire planned mission without further input from the pilot, turning, changing altitude and adjusting throttle settings and airspeed in order to keep to planned times. Turns made by the autopilot are carefully planned to minimize exposure to known hostile radars, carefully controlling the angle of bank.

The control column does not move when autopilot is engaged, and if the pilot moves it, he automatically engages the control stick steering mode, disabling the autopilot while he maneuvers. The autopilot will then hold the new attitude, heading or altitude, until directed to return to the planned mission.

This is perhaps fortunate, since flying at night is in itself a demanding and difficult business (as is any instrument flying). There is much scope for disorientation and confusion when visual cues become unreliable or confusing - for instance when stars in the sky and lights on the ground are similar enough to be confused. The important thing is to believe your flight instruments and to avoid head movements (especially rapid head movements) as far as is possible. In the F-117A this is impossible, since the flight instruments (including the basic instrument flying 'T') are not located centrally on the panel. To fly on instruments, the Stealth Fighter pilot must look to the left, while to change radio frequencies he must lean forward far enough for his head to tell him that his aircraft has rolled and climbed. Add in tiredness and fatigue, and it can be seen that flying the F-117A at low level, at night, by hand, could be a very dangerous business.

But at the same time, simply sitting back, hands off, and monitoring the various systems raises its own challenges. Without the task of physically flying the aircraft, it can be difficult to maintain concentration, and on long transits the seat can become very uncomfortable. For ferry flights through safe airspace, the pilot will sit on an air-filled plastic doughnut, much like a child's rubber

ESCAPING DETECTION

During the long transit to the target, the F-117A is not entirely invisible, and the pilot must remain alert to the presence of low cloud, moonlight, and cloud above his aircraft, in order to avoid being sighted visually by other aircraft or from the ground.

During high-altitude flight, with the precise altitudes differing according to the conditions, conventional aircraft can produce a conspicuous vapor trail (contrail), which acts as a giant arrow pointing to the exact position of the aircraft. One way to avoid this is to fly above or below the air in which contrails are forming, or alternatively, fuel additives can be used to reduce the size of the individual droplets of moisture within the trail. F-117As

routinely avoid flying at altitudes where contrail formation is likely, and may also use fuel additives, though this cannot be confirmed.

Even if the F-117A is effectively invisible to most types of radar, there is a problem with very low frequency radar, which can even detect the massive volume of turbulent air generated by the aircraft's passage through the sky. Some sources suggest that cruising speeds are optimized to minimize wake turbulence, and that flight plans also take account of high-level winds to reduce the size of the aircraft's 'wake'.

COL CHUCK GREER

ring, but to eject while sitting on one of these would be dangerous, since it would compress under acceleration. Other aids used on long ferry flights can also be used during long-range bombing missions however. Flight surgeons on the F-117A force are more than happy to prescribe the amphetamine Dexedrine though the pilots themselves prefer rock and roll played (very loud) on a Sony Walkman hooked up to the helmet. 'Piddlepacks' are also routinely carried, to relieve the pressure on bladders and kidneys.

Above: An F-117A pilot is illuminated by the green glow of his instruments and displays as he taxies out of his Canyon at Tonopah.

IR SIGNATURE

Although effectively invisible to many types of radar, the F-117A is visible to the naked eye, and to heat-detecting sensors. The aircraft's IR (Infra Red, or heat) signature is carefully managed and every effort is made to avoid 'hot spots'

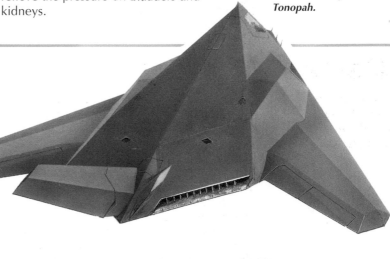

Right: The broad, flat exhausts of the F-117A spread the jet efflux out, giving it a larger surface area, which cools more rapidly than the conventional 'tight' cylinder of air produced by a conventional engine nozzle.

REFUELLING

The faceting which gives the F-117A its unique appearance and low observability also imposes limitations. The aircraft is not as aerodynamically efficient as it would have been had the fuselage been gracefully curved and faired, and it has been estimated that the sharp angles and multiple planes of the surface impose a fuel consumption penalty of about 20%. This is exacerbated by the unusual engine outlet design, which is less efficient than a conventional straight-through round jet pipe. The thrust and efficiency penalties imposed by the broad flat nozzles have not been publicly quantified, but certainly further degrade performance and range.

Above: Once the F-117A emerged from the 'Black World', it could refuel from any air force tanker, and was not limited to operating with specially selected crews from one Beale-based unit. The F-117A is a large aircraft for a single-seater, and is not dwarfed by the bulk of this 22nd ARW KC-10A Extender from March AFB, California.

This makes in-flight refuelling a vital part of F-117A operations, and a revolving in-flight refuelling receptacle was provided on the upper fuselage centreline, just behind the canopy. Like all USAF aircraft, the F-117A is equipped to receive fuel from a tanker with a rigid boom, rather than using a probe to engage a drogue on the end of a flexible hose trailed by a tanker, as favored by the US Navy, RAF, and most European air arms.

The probe and drogue method of in-flight refuelling demands little from the tanker crew, who simply stream one or more hoses, and maintain a pre-briefed flightpath while the aircraft requiring fuel plug in to the drogues. More than one aircraft can be refuelled at any one time, though the rate of flow from a single hose is considerably less than is possible through a solid boom. Moreover, refuelling is a very difficult business for the pilot of the receiver aircraft, who has to guide his probe (which may be offset to one side, and on some aircraft may not even be easily visible to him!) into a tiny drogue basket, which his own slipstream will tend to disturb and push this way and that. "Like trying to shove spaghetti up a wildcat's backside" is one common description of the procedure, while many pilots use the cruder aphorism, "it's like trying to take a running fuck at a

rolling doughnut." Missing the basket can have serious consequences, too. Probes can be easily damaged, as can the drogue baskets themselves. Add bad weather, turbulence and darkness, and in-flight refuelling can become both difficult and stressful.

The 'flying boom' method is less stressful for the receiver pilot, who simply maintains position below the tanker, while a dedicated operator (the boomer) uses aerodynamic control surfaces on the end of the boom to 'fly' its nozzle into the receiver aircraft's receptacle. Each method has its adherents, but the flying boom method is firmly entrenched within the US Air Force.

Simply finding the tanker is not easy for the F-117A pilot. Other tactical aircraft can use their own onboard radar to search for tankers, or can be guided towards the tanker by AWACS or friendly ground radar. Alternatively, tanker and receiver can use air-to-air TACAN (Tactical Aid to Navigation) and DME (Distance Measuring Equipment) to effect a rendezvous, but for the F-117, the procedure is usually less simple, and less co-operative. The pilot normally relies on finding the tankers autonomously, without radar emissions, using pinpoint navigation to find the tankers in their orbit. The F-117 formates off the tanker's starboard wingtip, dropping back to a pre-contact position 50 ft behind the tanker's extended refuelling boom, edging forward in response to signals conveyed by flashing lights. The procedure is completely radio silent.

To aid the boomer, the F-117A is fitted with a tiny light on the canopy apex, this shining aft to illuminate the in-flight refuelling receptacle. Normally, the 'boomer' would call the receiver aircraft forward, constantly updating the distance between the two aircraft in feet. But in the radio-silent world of the F-117A, the pilot of the Black Jet is responsible for getting himself into the contact position, referring to a yellow position stripe on the tanker's belly, and to the tanker's own lights. This is not easy, given the restricted upward visibility from the Black Jet's heavily-framed pyramidal canopy. Two sets of PDI (Pilot Direction Indicator) lights controlled by the boomer tell the pilot if he is too low or too high. Once in position, and steady, the F-117 pilot will see the tanker's boom extend hydraulically towards his aircraft's spine, but will have to crane his head down and forward if he wants to look up and see the boomer. He will hope for a successful contact first time. Without one he will have to drop back, approach again, and re-establish his position. A failed contact is stressful for the boomer, too. All boomers cleared to refuel the F-117 are carefully briefed on the delicacy of the aircraft's skin and it is a matter of some professional pride among boomers to avoid 'dinging it' with the boom tip.

But while the F-117As remain 'radio silent' during refuelling, they do extend their small radio antennas, ready to talk to the tanker pilot if something goes wrong, but above all waiting for the tanker to transmit the code

nominally operate in pairs.

The final refuelling will have been conducted as close as is safe to the enemy border, and, crossing this, the F-117A pilot conducts a brief 'Fence check', ensuring that position lights are off, aerials are retracted, that fuel is flowing correctly, and that sufficient fuel remains to get back to the tanker, outbound. Crossing into enemy airspace in the knowledge that one has not made the normal efforts to avoid enemy radar, the widely quoted reaction of one Black Jet pilot - "I hope this Stealth shit really works!" - seems entirely understandable.

Below: An F-117A seen plugged into a 9th SRW KC-135Q. The 9th SRW's KC-135Qs for many years performed the sensitive task of refuelling the USAF's SR-71 Blackbird spyplanes. The 'Beale Bandits' were a natural choice to provide tanker support to the F-117A when it was still a highly classified black world programme.

word that would mean that the mission was cancelled and that they were to return to base. Once hooked up to the boom, though, the pilot can talk to the boomer on intercom, without using radio.

When the first F-117A finishes refuelling, it moves to the tanker's port wing, stabilizing there while the second aircraft refuels. Once the second aircraft finishes refuelling it joins the first off the port wing and then, after more coded light flashing, both aircraft continue with their mission. Using the flying boom refuelling system meant that only one F-117A could refuel from a tanker at once. Usually operating in pairs, two F-117As would refuel from a single tanker, though more aircraft might stack up off the tanker's wing if tanker assets were scarce. Once he leaves the tanker, the F-117A pilot will be unlikely to see his wingman again, even though the aircraft

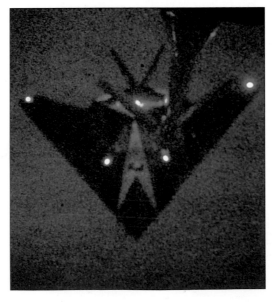

Left: On operations, an F-117A could approach the tanker without lights, though even those visible here would be virtually invisible to the naked eye, being visible primarily in the IR spectrum. Wingtip navigation lights are seen here, along with intake lights and the inflight refuelling receptacle light shining aft from the canopy apex. A faint glow can also be seen from the engine exhaust outlets.

ATTACK HEADING

The mission will almost certainly have been planned with frequent turns, these being flown by the autopilot in order to minimize exposure to hostile radar. If unexpected (mobile) radars are encountered the pilot will assess whether to fly around them or directly at them (frontal aspect stealthiness is the lowest of all on the F-117). Generally though, the pilot of the F-117A remains a systems monitor for most of the flight, which is flown hands-off by the autopilot.

At the final pre-IP turn point, the pilot (or more accurately the autopilot) will turn onto a new heading, probably the attack heading, and will continue to overfly the IP, descending to attack altitude if necessary. He will quickly check altitude, air speed and heading, and make sure that the computer is in the ATTACK mode. The altitude will depend on a number of factors, including atmospheric factors (which will affect the performance of the FLIR and DLIR), and the nature of the target. In a conventional aircraft, the pilot will be 'maxed out' during the IP-to-target run, alert to enemy air defenses and ready to take any evasive action necessary. The F-117A pilot should know that he is invulnerable, and, in theory at least, he concentrates on weapons delivery to the exclusion of all else. There is, reportedly, little of the 'pucker factor' encountered by generations of bomber pilots in previous wars. The pilot will switch from the navigation to the weapons delivery mode, arming the weapons, then switching the system to 'WEAPONS ARMED, OFF SAFE' to prevent accidental release.

As he passes the IP, the target itself will be the next waypoint, and the IRADS cross hairs will automatically position themselves over the target area selected by the computer. This far out, the cross hairs cover an area 'the size of two zip-codes', but the picture is rapidly refined as the target gets closer, and as the pilot fine-tunes the grain. For most of the flight the FLIR is usually locked forward, but as the aircraft approaches the target, the sensor is steered by the INS. Even in the wide 'Field of View' mode, the sensor's viewpoint is actually very narrow, and the INS therefore has to be extremely accurate in order to ensure that the target is within the sensor's field of regard. Once the target has been located in the wide field of view, the FLIR switches to its narrow field of view, with the cross hairs remaining centered over the target.

TARGETING SENSORS

The F-117A relies on self-designating for its laser-guided bombs, using a pair of combined FLIR/laser designator turrets above (FLIR) and below (DLIR) the nose. These form the Infra-Red Acquisition and Detection System (IRADS). The FLIR 'hands over' to the DLIR as the target passes below the nose.

FLIR turret

DLIR turret

Left: The presence of blade antennas above and below the fuselage indicate that this is a training mission. During operations, antennas are kept retracted, and the underfuselage red anti-collision light is not fitted. Even tiny protruberances like this dramatically increase the aircraft's radar cross section, and multiply the chance of detection.

Below: The F-117A spends most of its life at medium level, where it alone is almost immune from detection or interception. Altitude is determined by the requirements of the sensors, with lower altitudes being necessary in hazy or dusty conditions. Here an F-117A nears its practice target (a trash can filled with glowing coal) high over the Nevada desert, on a flight from Tonopah.

TARGET ACQUIRED

The sensors will actually acquire the target at between 10 and 15 miles, depending on atmospheric and weather conditions, and the pilot adjusts the IRADS gain to optimize target contrast. Meanwhile, the pilot simultaneously checks his altitude, heading and airspeed, and selects 'ARM' on the master armament switch. He compares the target in the cross hairs with the target photo on his kneeboard, and checks whether the cross hairs are correctly centered over the target. If they are not, he can slew them in any direction, using a small TD button on the throttles. Once he is happy that the cross hairs are over the exact aim point on the target, he presses and releases the TD button.

SENSOR TURRETS

The **IRADS** turrets each incorporated three apertures, one for the **FLIR**, one for the laser and one for a simple TV camera. The turrets were derived from those fitted to the Rockwell OV-10D Bronco.

The aim point may be a window or an air vent, or a precise point on a wall or roof, and is known as the DMPI (Designated Mean Point of Impact) The aim point is now locked-up, and will be automatically tracked. The laser fires to determine slant range. The F-117A's laser designator is part of the IRADS system, and is duplicated in the FLIR and DLIR turrets. It is the only non-passive piece of equipment on the aircraft and its use is thus carefully controlled. Unclassified reports would seem to suggest that the laser remains 'on' once it has fired to determine range, but this seems most unlikely. Rather, it seems

more probable that the laser fires occasionally to determine range, then fires briefly for a continuous period to illuminate the target after bomb release.

At some point, before the target 'disappears' under the nose, the FLIR automatically hands over to the DLIR. Many sources have cast doubts as to how this can be possible, since the DLIR does not appear to be able to look forward as far as the FLIR looks down, so there would appear to be a gap in coverage. In fact, at a point some way ahead of the aircraft, the FLIR and DLIR can see a target simultaneously. In order to achieve successful

hand-offs from the FLIR to the DLIR (and vice versa), the two turrets must be boresighted on the ground, by aligning both with the same target, simultaneously. To do this, the nose of the F-117A has to be raised by rolling the nosewheel up a 30-in ramp.

It may be that the DLIR turret can move back in its housing to squint forward along the belly of the aircraft, though this would seem difficult, even without the screen covering the turret. It may be that the FLIR can look down more steeply to the side than it can along the centerline, while the DLIR is offset to starboard, set into a sloping part of

the underside, allowing it to look further forward than is generally realized, especially out to starboard. If the F-117A approaches its target obliquely, there is certainly no gap in the coverage between the two turrets, but it is unclear as to whether the two sensors can be boresighted on a target directly in front of the aircraft. However it is achieved, there is a transition from FLIR to DLIR, and this is usually marked by a small 'jump' in the picture on the central display.

Above: The sensor turret is usually rotated with its windows facing aft, into the housing. The fine mesh screen is hardly visible.

MAKE READY

As he approaches the target, the F-117A pilot will start to make ready for dropping his weapons, which will inevitably be conventional 2,000 lb bombs, fitted with precision guidance kits which will allow them to 'home' onto laser energy reflected by the designated target.

Below: The F-117's RAM covering does not need to be black, and indeed the first prototype and early FSD aircraft were painted in a medium grey. This actually proved more effective as a night camouflage colour, black being too stark and too likely to produce a 'hard' silhouette. But after the SR-71 and U-2R, the USAF was determined that black was the right colour.

The F-117A can designate its own targets, illuminating a precise point with a laser slaved to the IR sensor. On the ground, the laser spot is approximately 12 to 18 inches in diameter. The seeker head of the bomb then 'looks' for reflected laser energy of the right frequency, and the bomb guides itself onto the illuminated point. All the F-117A pilot has to do is to monitor that the cross hairs of the designator are centered on the target, intervening only to make minor adjustments, if necessary. This system is simple to use, even in a single-seat attack aircraft, and gives remarkable accuracy.

The watching world gasped at the DLIR image of a 2,000 lb LGB going straight down a one yard wide vent in the so-called AT&T building in the heart of Baghdad on the first night of Operation Desert Storm. It was great television, but to the pilots of the Black Jet this was little more than routine. Years before,

during the long black years at Tonopah, Stealth pilots had been used to nominating specific windows in certain motels as their 'targets' during long range training missions. They expected a level of accuracy which would allow them to put a bomb through a particular window, or down a particular airshaft. And during Desert Storm, almost nine out of ten bombs dropped by the F-117 hit with similar accuracy, while the best other aircraft types could manage was a 'hit rate' (against less 'pinpoint' targets) of about 30%.

Such a degree of accuracy is not just good for spectacular imagery on the TV news, of course. The ability to put a bomb reliably on target within feet allows the F-117A to knock out bunkers and hardened facilities, with a second bomb exploiting the weaknesses caused by a first weapon. In attacks against underground bunkers, for example, an initial bomb might penetrate the first couple of levels, with a second punching down to the heart of the complex. In the post Cold War world, accuracy also allows devastating attacks against legitimate targets with a minimum of collateral damage, and with minimal impact on the 'innocent' civil populace.

Above and right: Two views of Tonopah-based F-117As on training flights over Nevada and California during the early days of the programme. The F-117A's faceted exterior was dictated by the inability of Lockheed mathematicians to work out the RCS of a shape composed of compound curves. With increased computer power, this became possible, and aircraft like the B-2 and F-22 do not need to be faceted.

RISKING THE "GOLDEN BB"

The ability to penetrate hostile defenses 'unseen', together with the proven ability to strike with the utmost precision, inevitably means that the F-117A will be assigned the most difficult targets. Tonight, our target must be hit within two seconds of the TOT (Time over target) detailed on the ATO (Air Task Order). Several aircraft will be hitting several targets simultaneously. If one bomb impacts early, it will alert the defenses that something is happening, and the enemy defenses will put up a wall of AAA, perhaps even blind-launching SAMs. And while the intense fire will be unaimed, there is always the chance that some enemy gunner will 'get lucky'. But until the bombs hit, the enemy are not even aware that there are Stealth Fighters in the area.

In larger-scale attacks, the F-117A force might have to hit targets in the same area in waves, or one aircraft might wake up the defenses with its first bomb, then drop its second weapon on another target a few moments later. During the Gulf War, pilots of the Black Jet frequently found themselves flying through a barrage of unaimed flak. Fortunately, none were hit, though it was nevertheless an extremely scary business. There are, of course, ways and means of stacking the odds in our favor. If a first bomb wakes up the defenses, then the next aircraft might fly in between six and twenty minutes later, depending on the fire discipline of the enemy gunners. They will have been firing constantly for some five minutes, and will inevitably stop for a couple of minutes to allow their gun barrels to cool down. If the next aircraft flies in before those barrels have cooled properly, their accuracy will be significantly affected.

At the end of the day, if you are the guy sitting in the cockpit, then it doesn't matter if the guy on the ground can see you or not. A 57-mm shell hitting your airplane will do exactly the same damage if it hits you, whether it was deliberately aimed or just a lucky break. The chance is always there that your wingman's bomb might wake the defenses, or that a particularly lucky or skilled radar operator might connect that tiny return among the clutter with an F-117A and might be able to trigger the blind defensive barrage. The fact that Stealth Fighters came through 43 days of the Gulf War unscathed isn't necessarily much comfort. If it's a chance shot that's going to get you, and if they were lucky enough to avoid that one freak shot, that one 'golden BB' with F-117A engraved upon it, then it is natural to wonder whether surely the odds might not be shortening. So even if the skies around you are quiet as you fly your final IP to target attack run, that might change before you actually release your bomb, and the brief moments closest to the target are naturally stressful.

Most F-117A pilots who have seen action would admit to being nervous in the target area, but equally, most would confirm that they were less nervous than perhaps they expected. Certainly, a SAM launch didn't engender the bowel-loosening terror it might if you were flying an F-16 (say) nor did it require violent evasive action or countermeasures. But the first time a SAM is coming up at you, not to react, and to go on flying along serenely is difficult enough. You know that the missile won't lock on to you, but there will always be doubts and 'What ifs'. If it couldn't happen, you wouldn't have trained so hard, and would not have practiced specific maneuvers to defeat different types of missile. Pilots are aware of the times in the history of the program when radar was suddenly able to see the F-117A or the 'Have Blue' or a model on a pole; when the sudden increase in signature was caused by fasteners that had suddenly projected a few thousandths of an inch from the otherwise smooth skin, or even when the performance of a particular facet had been destroyed through contamination by bird droppings. In the F-117A, even a minor birdstrike (which you might not even feel, if it was in a non-critical area) could easily quadruple your radar cross section.

Luckily, the Gulf War gave plenty of reassuring experiences, and these have entered the folklore of the Stealth community. En route from one Baghdad target to another, Capt. Matt Byrd suddenly saw two bright white flashes off the right wing. Looking out, Byrd was close enough to see that the lights were SAM rocket motors illuminating the ground and the control vans around them as they launched. The SA-3s initially looked as if they were guiding, but passed harmlessly behind the aircraft, exploding far enough away to cause the young pilot no problems. Generally, experience has taught pilots of the Black Jet that SAMs are not to be feared, but an unaimed wall of flak remains potentially dangerous.

But the IP to target run is no time for nerves, nor indeed for any extraneous thoughts. There are weapon selections to be made and procedures to be followed. So as he flies in towards the target at a steady 480 kts, the pilot will have to concentrate, and he will have to ignore the distraction of AAA (which may be heard as a series of pops, if it is close enough), or the potential for AAA. Many pilots actually make a deliberate decision to keep their heads inside the cockpit, ignoring the outside world entirely, and focusing only on the job in hand. Some even lower the ejection seat by a few inches.

Above: A pair of GBU-27s topple from the weapons bays of an F-117A. AAA bursts harmlessly behind the aircraft, the gunners having received inadequate warning.

BOMB DOORS OPEN

With the DMPI locked-up, the F-117 pilot flies on towards the target, perhaps making minor corrections to adjust for crosswind as steering cues come up in the HUD and MFD. With no wind, the attack remains 'hands off'. With the laser measuring range, the computer will eventually generate 'within range' symbology in the HUD and on the MFD, and if the pilot agrees he presses the pickle button on the stick. This does not necessarily release the weapon, however, since in the normal attack mode, the pilot's selection has merely given his consent to the attack, and the computer then selects the optimum time for bomb release, taking into account the wind, airspeed, and the bomb's ballistic characteristics and predicted trajectory.

Below: A GBU-27 is manoeuvred below an F-117A, for loading into the port weapons bay. The Paveway III guidance kit is not fitted.

The bomb doors open with a 'clunk' that can be heard and felt in the cockpit, and then snap shut when the bomb is clear. As they open, the aircraft begins to vibrate, as air buffets into the weapons bays, and DOORS OPEN warning lights blaze into life on the

instrument panel, telling the pilot that he's suddenly lost much of his invisibility. Because they open to a vertical position, open bomb doors present a marvellous radar target. For every second that the bomb doors are open, the F-117A has effectively lost its invisibility to enemy radar. With them open, the F-117A's radar cross section is huge, much like that of a conventional fighter, and the aircraft is thus briefly potentially vulnerable to hostile fire. The doors therefore stay open for the minimum possible period, usually closing before an enemy radar will have made a single sweep. There have been reports that bomb door opening is actually linked to the RHAWS (Radar Homing And Warning System), which prevent opening if the aircraft is being 'painted' by a hostile radar.

Above: An inert GBU-27A/B falls from the open bay of Scorpion 5' (784), the last of the FSD F-117As. Test cameras are fitted in faceted fairings below the aircraft's wings. In the early days, weapons were dropped from the extended trapeze, but these are now cleared to be dropped straight from the weapons bays. The aircraft has a well-patched appearance.

Right: Groundcrew secure a GBU-27 to the starboard trapeze. The aircraft appears to be fitted with the newer, composite bomb bay doors. The GBU-27 (this one is still without its control fins fitted) is basically a BLU-109 penetrator fitted with a Paveway III seeker and the smaller Paveway II tail.

LASER LOCK ON

The laser will keep locked onto the target, but will fire briefly before impact to illuminate and designate the target. The DLIR turret moves slightly in its gimballed mount to keep the laser pointing directly at the target, 'steered' by the auto-tracker. Inside the cockpit, the pilot watches the central IRADS display, monitoring that the cross hairs remain centered on the DMPI, ready to make corrections if they do not. The pilot may suddenly see the bomb appear in the bottom of the display, and may see it streak into the DMPI. He will certainly see the target explode, with doors blowing out of bunkers to mark the success of the attack.

Top: When the F-117 emerged from the Black World, its operating unit was able to adopt a formal frontline fighter wing identity. Accordingly, the 4450th Tactical Group became the 37th Tactical Fighter Wing. A handful of aircraft wear large tailcodes reflecting the wing and individual squadron identities.

In most circumstances, the defenses will be unaware of his presence until now, and it would be typical that AAA would begin to explode behind him, as he egresses. Happiness is AAA in your rear-view mirror!

The F-117A normally delivers its bombs from straight and level flight, there being little need for the accuracy of a dive attack using LGBs (which are inherently accurate anyway) and with no need to loft the bombs in order to avoid overflying the target. Loft attacks are possible however, and software has been developed to allow the technique to be used, though a dive for speed and pull-up to loft will typically require three handovers back and forth between the FLIR and DLIR.

The Stealth Fighter's complete reliance on infrared sensors for target acquisition and tracking is the key to its invulnerability in the target area. If the F-117A pilot had to use

radar, its emissions would be detected (and could be pinpointed). It would be like using a torch in a dark room. Even if you don't shine the torch at your enemy, he can see exactly where you are. But at the same time, electro-optical and IR sensors impose their own limitations. The most serious of these limitations is the aircraft's almost total inability to drop bombs in anything but clear weather. During the Gulf war, huge numbers of F-117A missions were scrubbed due to poor weather over the target, and yet more ended with the aircraft being forced to drop on secondary targets, or even bringing their bombs home.

If you can't see the target, you can't hit it. And if you can't see your secondary target either, you'll have to take your bombs home, or jettison them in some pre-designated safe area. Even if you can see the target, the thinnest layer of wispy cloud can be enough to make your bomb miss the DMPI, as it disrupts laser designation. The vulnerability of the F-117A's IRADS was demonstrated conclusively during the Gulf War. Successful missions frequently hid some alarming shortfalls. Amid the celebrations surrounding the first night attacks it went barely unnoticed that of 60 bombs carried to their targets, only 49 were dropped, and of the 49 bombs dropped, only 28 actually hit their aim

Right: The small fairings aft of the star and bar each contain a radar reflector. These are fitted on training missions to allow the aircraft to be tracked by ATC.

points! Even ignoring the bombs that were not dropped, this represented only a 55% hit rate, while F-111s scored a 70% hit rate on the same night. (F-111s, of course, would not have performed so well over Baghdad, and many might have been lost to AAA and SAMs.) The third wave of eight aircraft performed particularly badly, scoring only five hits because of a bank of cloud which rolled in, obscuring many targets. On the second night, things went slightly better. Of 48 bombs put into the air, 23 direct hits were recorded. But poor weather on the third night allowed only six hits, with 17 hits on the fourth and fifth nights.

Weather conditions were 'perfect' on 21/22 January, but even then, two misses (of 28 bombs dropped) were recorded by the second wave. When F-117As attacked Tu-16 bombers in their revetments at Al Taqaddum, only three of the eight bombers were destroyed, leaving five survivors, which fortunately failed to carry out their planned chemical warfare mission. On 24/25 January, a strike against HASs at Kirkuk and Qayyara West proved completely fruitless. A wave of ten F-117As scored no less than 19 no-drops, with the single bomb actually dropped scoring a miss. Another mission, against Tigris and Euphrates bridges, conducted by twelve F-117As the previous night, scored the all-time record low of 23 no-drops.

It would be too easy to overstate the F-117A's unreliability in poor weather conditions. The fact remains that the aircraft was and is capable of operating in airspace in which other bombers would suffer unacceptably heavy losses. Moreover, the F-117A's invisibility to radar allowed it to attack targets with the advantage of total surprise. Again and again, targets attacked by the Black Jet have received no warning until bombs actually explode, when it is often too late to respond. On 19 January 1991, the USAF sent a force of 32 F-16 'bombers' against the Baghdad Nuclear Research Center (also known as Osirak), supported by 16 F-15 escort fighters, four EF-111 jammers, eight F-4G SEAD aircraft and eleven KC-135 tankers. The Iraqis ignited smoke pots, which completely obscured the target, and the raid caused no significant damage, while two of the F-16s were shot down. On the night of

21/22 January, eight F-117s attacked the same target, giving the defenders no warning and successfully destroying three reactors and badly damaging the fourth. They required only two KC-135 tankers for support.

Below: The F-117A's exhausts are only visible from above and behind. Flow straighteners are just visible from this angle.

EGRESS AND RETURN

There is a natural tendency to relax, just a little, after you leave the target area, though in many ways the egress and return home may be the most dangerous part of the flight. While radar is no more likely to see you outbound as it was while you were inbound, the enemy now knows that you are in his airspace, and probably has a reasonable idea of the general direction in which you are heading. If the Stealth Fighter's invisibility to radar is combat-proven, many are less sanguine about the aircraft's ability to evade some other sensors. When a larger Northrop B-2 bomber visited the Farnborough air show in late 1996, Rapier SAM crews had no difficulty acquiring and tracking the aircraft using electro-optical and infrared equipment, and while the F-117 does incorporate many features to reduce its IR signature, there may be a danger if an IRSTS (Infra Red Search and Track) equipped fighter gets close enough for its equipment to deal with a low-signature target.

Above: The return from the target is no time to relax. The F-117A is as invisible to friendly radars as it is to those of the enemy, and the risk of collision is not insignificant. Tracks and timings have to be carefully planned and adhered to.

But the enemy may sometimes be the least of a pilot's worries. The Standard Operating Procedure for the F-117A demands that the pilot remains radio silent, and the returning F-117A is as invisible to friendly forces as it is to the enemy. In crowded airspace (as was often the case when aircraft were returning from targets during Desert Storm) the risk of collision is considerable, and inbound and outbound timings and tracks had to be very carefully co-ordinated, with pinpoint navigational accuracy continuing to be

completely vital. The journey home is thus no time to relax.

In Desert Storm, particularly after the enemy air defenses had been degraded by constant bombing, F-117A pilots did make a brief call to the AWACS as they egressed, letting the sector controller that they were outbound, that they were friendlies, and not to send anyone after them!

During a long bombing campaign (as was conducted during Desert Storm), there is a natural tendency to become more blasé during later missions. But the wise F-117A pilot never relaxes his vigilance, since there is nothing to guarantee that the enemy will not eventually strike lucky and field a new sensor that might detect the aircraft, or there might be a minor technical glitch that robs the aircraft of some of its cloak of invisibility. But having found and attacked the target, and with the autopilot guiding the aircraft inexorably towards the tanker rendezvous, the cockpit workload is reduced, and there is time for thought, or even food! Returning from his first mission of the Gulf War, Al Whitley ate half a Snickers bar, forbidding himself the second half in punishment for missing his second aim point. It would be rare for many pilots to return with half a chocolate bar, had they set themselves the same rules. It is simply unusual not to get a direct hit when flying the Black Jet.

Once back over friendly territory, the first priority is to find the post-strike tanker, and to take on sufficient fuel to return to base. During the Gulf War, the F-117As were often very low on fuel as they egressed, having made deep penetrations of enemy airspace, only to struggle home against severe headwinds. Without radar, air-to-air TACAN and with radio silence being maintained, finding the tanker at all is by no means straightforward, and relies (as does so much in the F-117A world) on navigational accuracy and split-second timing. All of the factors which made refuelling difficult on the outbound journey make it just as difficult on the way home, but with the added problems of fatigue: the pilot may feel less 'psyched-up', perhaps even with some feelings of anticlimax. And if you missed the tanker on the way to the target, you could abort the mission and still have sufficient fuel to return to base. On the way home, you are refuelling in order to be able to get home. If for any reason you can't refuel, you may not reach a friendly airfield at all. As if all this were not enough, the tanker may fly a racetrack pattern, banking at angles of up to 15°, which can cause spatial disorientation, especially in poor weather.

Above: One F-117A flies on as its wingman breaks away. The F-117A's distinctive arrow-head planform is a unique shape in the sky. Such formation flying is rare in the F-117A, and the Stealth Fighter's cockpit is a lonely place. On operations, the pilot does not use his radio, flies with no wingman and seldom sees another aircraft.

Left: The F-117A relies on split-second timing and pinpoint navigation to find its targets, and to find the inflight refuelling tanker. The aircraft usually remains radio-silent, and this imposes a high workload on the pilot.

LANDING

During the early days at Tonopah, F-117A pilots would shoot practice instrument approaches until they got down to 2,000 lb of fuel, and then land. The F-117 has ILS, using retractable horizontal antennae immediately behind the cockpit. After an operational mission, the F-117A would land straight away.

With no flaps, the F-117A comes in flat and fast, and consequently needs a long runway to operate from. The actual approach attitude is 9.5 a (9.5 units, Angle of Attack), giving a reasonably normal sink rate, but with a fast landing speed of around 150 knots. The aircraft doesn't actually have to slow down that much from its normal cruising speed, so a flashy, high g fighter-pilot run-in and break is not required. This is probably just as well, since at night, with the restricted visibility from the Black Jet's tiny cockpit windows, such a maneuver would be somewhat disorientating. A normal approach can be disorientating enough to a tired pilot, since under some conditions a reversed image of the runway can appear as a reflection at the top of the screen. Despite this, and despite the high landing speed, most pilots rate the aircraft as being easier to land than the F-16.

The brakes are powerful (and much improved by comparison with the brakes fitted to the first F-117s delivered), but use of the Pioneer Aerospace braking parachute is still routine. The 18-ft diameter brake chute is deployed as soon as the nosewheel touches

the runway: it is actuated by pulling on a T-handle mounted beside the right-hand display screen and streams from a compartment between the tailfin roots. Brake-chute operation is not entirely straightforward, especially in a crosswind when it can foul on the roots of the tailfins. Actuation is therefore practiced during a high-speed taxi run even before the trainee Stealth pilot makes his official first flight. The chute is usually black, like the aircraft, and is a vital piece of equipment. It is used except in the strongest crosswinds. Without it, the early aircraft (with Loral steel brakes) needed a rollout of more than 10,000 ft to avoid seriously over-heating the brakes. The stopping distance with the new carbon-carbon brakes is slightly shorter, but if they are used without the brake chute, the aircraft must sit stationary in a 'hot brake area' for one minute after rolling off the runway, for the brakes to cool down. The fire risk is significant. In some circumstances 10,000 ft of runway may not always be available, and the aircraft is fitted with an airfield arrester hook, a lightweight device intended to prevent the aircraft from running off the end of a runway in the event of a brake failure. The aircraft must already be travelling fairly slowly to engage typical airfield arrester-wire equipment. The hook is mounted in a separate bay, behind a fully RAM sealed door: this has to be jettisoned explosively if the hook is used.

Below: An F-117A lands at Lockheed's Palmdale plant, black brake chute full streamed even before the nosewheel is on the runway, and before the main gear oleos are fully compressed.

Above: The position of the F-117A's brake parachute bay makes it easy to wrap the chute around the aircraft's fins, and the device cannot be used in anything more than a moderate crosswind. The trainee F-117A pilot taxies the aircraft and deploys the chute before his first solo flight.

Right: An F-117A on final approach to Tonopah, passing the off-base accomodation complex, oleos fully extended. The aircraft is fitted with ILS, with retractable horizontal antennas immediately aft of the cockpit.

DEBRIEFING

The F-117A taxies in much like any other tactical aircraft, though its pilots are more used to doing so on blacked-out airfields, using FLIR and guided by groundcrew with torches. At Tonopah the purpose-built shelters had doors at each end, and the aircraft could thus taxi into its assigned hangar (or canyon) from the back, so that it was facing forward when it started its next mission. The pilot would shut down in the canyon, but might leave electrical power on while the groundcrew connected up external power. If the aircraft was destined to fly again that day the INS would not be turned off, since realignment is so time-consuming. Alighting from the cockpit the pilot would briefly tell the crew chief of any defects or incidents that had occurred during the flight, before being driven to the operations building for debriefing.

During the Gulf War, the pilot would typically retrieve the arming lanyards (which pulled the pins and armed the fuses) from the weapons bay, these being prized souvenirs. One, or perhaps both, would then be handed to the groundcrew with a handshake and a grin which said more than words ever could. The groundcrew would plug their own equipment into the single-point diagnostic interface panel, which hinges down from the underside of the port wing.

F-117A debriefings tend to be fairly routine. The aircraft seldom diverge from their planned flight, and usually the only useful information

to emerge is the pilot's assessment of how his bombs behaved (though intelligence will examine his DLIR picture on video) and his reports as to the position and intensity of enemy AAA and SAMs. Nevertheless, the pilot will sit down with the squadron intelligence officer postflight (or with an Instructor following a routine training mission) and go through the mission in some detail. Video tape of the IRADS display is available immediately, greatly assisting damage assessment and attack effectiveness. Watching the tapes takes on an entirely different dimension after a no-kidding operational sortie. During the Gulf War, the aircraft's crew chief and other maintainers typically came into the debrief to watch the tapes, too, often bringing popcorn! The Stealth Fighter force remains a small, tight-knit and elite group, and there is a high level of camaraderie among all ranks. During Desert Storm, one pilot became known for bringing his groundcrew Apple Pie à la mode if he'd had a good night, stepping it up until he was taking apple pie and ice cream for some 200 maintenance troops!

Four F-117As lined up at Holloman AFB, shortly after the 37th FW moved to the New Mexico base and took over the identity of the 49th FW. The aircraft wear the tail markings of the 9th, 8th, and 7th Fighter Squadrons, with the furthest aircraft wearing 49th FW tail markings.

A FUTURE FOR STEALTH?

Many suspected that faceted Stealth aircraft like the F-117A would only ever be an interim step, necessitated because calculating radar returns from three-dimensional shapes was simply too difficult. There was plenty of evidence to suggest that smooth and blended curvaceous aircraft could have low radar cross sections. The original Northrop XB-49 flying wing proved extremely difficult to track on radar, while the F-16 and SR-71 both enjoyed lower radar cross sections than had once been predicted. The NASA Lifting Bodies (precursors to the Space Shuttle) proved similarly difficult to track on radar. Improved computer power allowed work on truly three-dimensional shapes, and this led to the second generation of 'curvy' Stealth aircraft, including the Northrop B-2 and Tacit Blue.

When Lockheed first invented their faceted 'Hopeless Diamond' configuration, the company believed that the configuration was equally applicable to large and small aircraft, and that radar cross section was a function of getting the facets right, and not of size. Following the success of the 'Have Blue' XSTs, Lockheed submitted two stealth aircraft based on the same configuration. One was a fighter-sized attack aircraft, the other much larger,

broadly equivalent to the F-111, with a crew of two, a 10,000 lb payload and a 3,600 nm range. The company was awarded a contract to build five FSD and 15 production examples of the fighter-sized aircraft, although its figures suggested that the larger 'bomber' would have had no greater a radar signature.

There would have been advantages in commissioning Lockheed to produce both the fighter-sized Stealth aircraft and the bomber,

Above: The rollout of 88-0843, the last of 59 production F-117As accepted by the US Air Force, delivered on 12 July 1990, and operational in the Gulf War as 'Affectionately Christine', flying 33 combat missions.

Left: Stealth Fighter is a misnomer for the F-117A, since the aircraft's sole purpose is to drop bombs. But the Stealth Bomber is this Leviathan, the Northrop B-2, which represents the next generation of stealth configuration, with a smoothly blended shape of complex curves which have the same affect as the F-117's facets.

Above: Optimised as a BVR interceptor, the Lockheed F-22 Raptor (seen here in YF-22 prototype form) incorporates considerable stealth technology. The USAF is desperately keen to safeguard funding for this, its next generation fighter, and may even use a derivative as an F-117A replacement.

since there was a need for both types of aircraft. The bomber would fulfil a USAF requirement for an Advanced Technology Bomber designed to penetrate hostile airspace without detection, and to hunt and attack mobile targets, primarily mobile ICBMs. It was clear that Low Observable technology would be crucial in allowing the aircraft to operate undetected and unmolested as it performed its role. A competition was launched in 1978, attracting proposals from a Northrop/Boeing team, and from a Lockheed/Rockwell team: though the size of the required ATB grew (largely at the urging of the commander of Air Force Systems Command), until it was a four-engined monster in broadly the same class as the B-58 Hustler, with expanded payload and a 6,000 mile unrefuelled range.

Lockheed dropped its faceted, highly swept F-117A type configuration at this point and unwittingly began work on a flying wing configuration very similar to that which Northrop were simultaneously working on. The difference was primarily one of size, since Lockheed listened to SAC insiders who advised small and short range to keep the price down, while Northrop listened to people inside the Pentagon, who urged them to maximize range at the expense of size and cost. The larger Northrop aircraft could have larger wing control surfaces, and was able to dispense with a tailfin, which the smaller Lockheed design needed. This made the Northrop design markedly more fuel efficient. Although the Lockheed aircraft demonstrated better radar cross section figures, the

Northrop bomber design was selected for production, supposedly 'on technical merit'. The more relaxed and slightly later timescale followed for the ATB allowed the winning team to make use of the new generation of Cray super computers, which were powerful enough to allow Ufimtsev's equations to be applied to predicting the RCS of three-dimensional shapes. This in turn allowed the resulting aircraft to have a more conventional aerodynamically smooth shape.

Above all, the USAF were concerned not to have all their eggs in one 'Stealthy' basket, and accepted a later deployment date for the bomber in order to take advantage of new technologies, and to ensure that Lockheed did not gain an effective monopoly in the new technology. The ATB program was never as secret as the Stealth Fighter program, primarily because the aircraft had an admissible Cold War role and was not intended for 'Special Forces' type operations.

The end of the Cold War marked a dramatic change in the B-2's fortunes, with planned procurement slashed from an original total of 132 aircraft (at $480 m each!) in four full-strength Bomb Wings, to a single two-squadron Bomb Wing of only 20 B-2s (at $2.2 bn each!), 16 of them operational at any one time. A program was quickly initiated to allow the aircraft to carry and drop conventionally armed PGMS, its initial role having been seen as being primarily nuclear.

Above: The B-2 is so expensive ($2.2 bn per aircraft) that only 20 will ever be procured. It is rapidly assuming a conventional, precision strike role.

F-117 VARIANTS

The emergence of the more aerodynamically efficient streamlined Stealth aircraft sounded the death knell for the faceted shape pioneered by the F-117A, although a number of advanced F-117A derivatives have been proposed by Lockheed in recent years, their attraction being one of swift, low-risk development and battle-proven effectiveness.

The designation F-117A+ was applied in-house to an ambitious upgrade of existing F-117A airframes. A prototype conversion was priced at $79 m, though exact details of the upgrade were not released. The F-117A+ may have been similar to the F-117 variant reportedly offered to the British Royal Air Force, which had revised B-2 type intakes and a clear-view F-22 type canopy, but which otherwise retained the basic configuration of the original F-117A. The USAF was reportedly more interested in this upgrade than in acquiring any new-build F-117 derivative.

When re-opening the F-117A production line was mooted, following the Gulf War, General McPeak, USAF Chief of Staff, was reportedly lukewarm, stating that he "wouldn't spend any money on what amounts to obsolete technology". Lockheed suggestions that the aircraft would make an ideal replacement for the F-4G in the Wild Weasel role were not taken up, and the USAF

F-117 - ADVANCED DERIVATIVES

The F-117 has spawned a number of advanced derivatives, offering improved performance, payload, range and versatility, though in the present funding climate these remain unbuilt. Shown here are the F-117B and the proposed 'F-117' also confusingly referred to as the F-117B for the British Royal Air Force.

F-117B (A/F-117X AND F-117N SIMILAR)

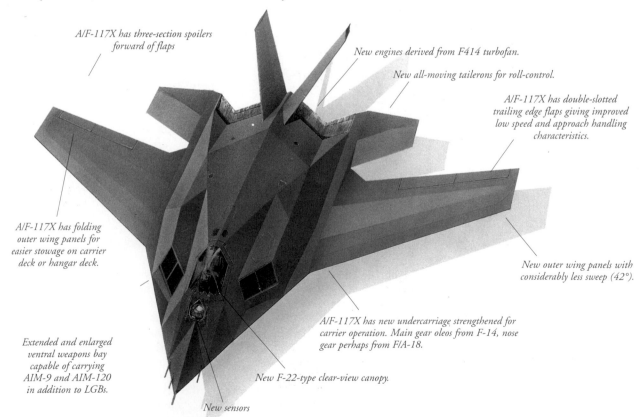

A/F-117X has three-section spoilers forward of flaps

New engines derived from F414 turbofan.

New all-moving tailerons for roll-control.

A/F-117X has double-slotted trailing edge flaps giving improved low speed and approach handling characteristics.

A/F-117X has folding outer wing panels for easier stowage on carrier deck or hangar deck.

New outer wing panels with considerably less sweep (42°).

A/F-117X has new undercarriage strengthened for carrier operation. Main gear oleos from F-14, nose gear perhaps from F/A-18.

Extended and enlarged ventral weapons bay capable of carrying AIM-9 and AIM-120 in addition to LGBs.

New F-22-type clear-view canopy.

New sensors

instead received dedicated F-16s.

A new-build advanced F-117 was offered to the USAF under the designation F-117B, this reportedly having considerable commonality with the navalized A/F-117X variant described below. The F-117B was credited with an MTOW of 73,200 lb (compared with 52,500 lb for the F-117A), with unrefuelled combat radius extended from 570 nm (1055 km) to 980 nm (1813 km), and with internal payload doubled to 10,000 lb. The F-117B might also feature new all-weather sensors, improved low observability, afterburning General Electric F414 engines and aerodynamic improvements.

Lockheed first proposed a navalized version of the F-117 to the US Navy following the cancellation of the AF/X strike aircraft, suggesting a 'Silver Bullet' force of between 40 and 75 aircraft. As originally conceived the F-117N had an off-the-shelf ACLS (Automatic Carrier Landing System) and some structural improvements to withstand the rigors of carrier landings and the corrosion-prone maritime environment. This proved

insufficiently attractive to deflect the Navy from its intended purchase of second-generation F/A-18 Hornets. Lockheed further refined the F-117N into the A/F-117X, which proved more interesting to the Navy, but which has still not been procured. The A/F-117X retains the basic body of the F-117, but has new wings, of slightly reduced sweep, and a separate conventional horizontal tailplane. The wings are foldable to allow the aircraft to use carrier elevators and hangar decks, and are fitted with extensive double-slotted trailing edge flaps to improve approach handling characteristics and reduce landing speed.

The new variant has a new, strengthened landing gear (perhaps taken directly from the F-14), with a redesigned nose unit, with twin nosewheels and a catapult tie bar. The aircraft is fitted with a new clear-view canopy, similar to that fitted to the F-22. Lockheed have reportedly suggested that the A/F-117X would be compatible with the AIM-120 AMRAAM, inferring that an air-to-air radar capability would be incorporated.

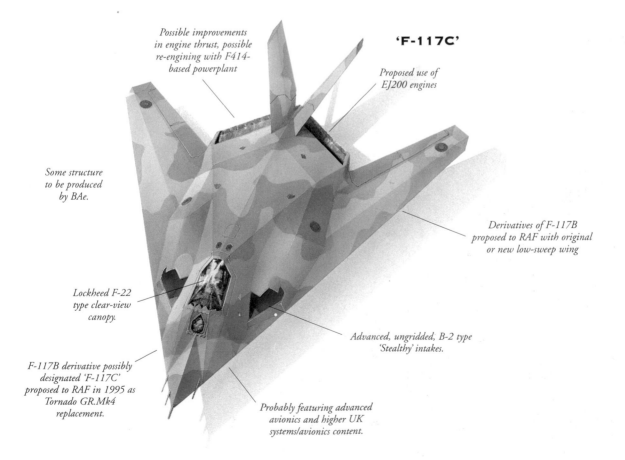

Possible improvements in engine thrust, possible re-engining with F414-based powerplant

'F-117C'

Proposed use of EJ200 engines

Some structure to be produced by BAe.

Derivatives of F-117B proposed to RAF with original or new low-sweep wing

Lockheed F-22 type clear-view canopy.

Advanced, ungridded, B-2 type 'Stealthy' intakes.

F-117B derivative possibly designated 'F-117C' proposed to RAF in 1995 as Tornado GR.Mk4 replacement.

Probably featuring advanced avionics and higher UK systems/avionics content.

SOMETHING BLACK IN THE SKY

In today's budgetary climate, however, funding for any new aircraft is difficult, and the F-117's success in the 'White World' makes it difficult to develop a low rate production, 'Black' derivative. As funding constraints become increasingly difficult, the USAF is concentrating more and more on its key core programs (particularly the F-22). The Northrop B-2, which represented the logical extrapolation of the Stealth idea, has been cut back dramatically, and it will represent little more than a limited 'Silver Bullet' force.

Right: An F-117A in flight over the fringes of the White Sands National Monument, close to its base at Holloman AFB, New Mexico, a suitably spectacular and awe-inspiring home for this remarkable strike aircraft.

Below: The all-aspect low-observability pioneered by the F-117A remains unusual, though low frontal RCS is becoming a design driver for many fighters.

It is difficult to predict the longer-term future for Stealth aircraft. Advances in radar technology and the use of alternative sensors will erode the advantage they currently enjoy, although broad signature management will remain an issue in combat aircraft design. Frontal radar cross section is now a key factor in the design of fighters and interceptors, but the kind of all-aspect low-observability typified by the F-117A has a more limited application. It would be foolish to dismiss the possibility of another strike aircraft optimized for radar stealth, but at the same time, it is probably realistic to assume that such a specialized platform would probably be another 'Skunk Works' type product, procured in tiny numbers and used for 'Special Forces' type roles. A 'cottage industry' has grown up around the investigation of Stealth aircraft, US Black programs, and the work carried out at Tonopah and Groom Lake. Unfortunately, the whole subject has become closely associated with that of UFOs, and specifically of the secret use of alien technology by the US Government, and this kind of hokum casts doubt on the veracity of other rumored Stealthy Black projects, from the Northrop (?) TR-3A tactical reconnaissance aircraft to the strategic high Mach SR-71 replacement, the Lockheed Aurora, and a host of other weird and wonderful strike and reconnaissance aircraft, from the 'Artichoke' to the Northrop A-17, a swing-wing strike derivative of the YF-23.

But as one former F-117A pilot opined, "When you strip away all this X-Files bullshit, it does seem kind of likely that there's something going on at Tonopah, and that someone is using our old facilities. I'm sure there's something black in the skies over Nevada." Whether or not he's right, at the moment, the F-117A remains the most capable and least vulnerable precision strike asset available to USAF commanders.